EXPECTANT CREATIVITY:

The Action of Hope in Christian Ethics

VINCENT J. GENOVESI, S.J.

SAINT JOSEPH'S UNIVERSITY
PHILADELPHIA

Imprimi Potest:
    Joseph P. Whelan, S.J.
    Provincial: Maryland Province of the Society of Jesus

Nihil Obstat:
    James McGrath
    Censor Librorum

Imprimatur:
    John Cardinal Krol
    Archbishop of Philadelphia
    February, 1982

The Nihil Obstat and Imprimatur simply indicate that a book is considered to be free from doctrinal or moral error. It is not implied that those who have granted the Nihil Obstat and Imprimatur agree with the contents, opinions or statements expressed.

DEDICATION

To my mother and father, in appreciation
of the faith that has guided me,
the hope that has calmed me,
the love that has strengthened me,
in ways that are gratefully remembered.

ACKNOWLEDGMENTS

The author is most grateful to Professor Jürgen Moltmann for his kind permission to quote from two of his books:

Religion, Revolution, and The Future, trans. M. Douglas Meeks; Charles Scribner's Sons, copyright © 1969 by Jürgen Moltmann.

Theology of Hope, copyright © 1967 by SCM Press Ltd. and Harper & Row, Publishers; English translation by James W. Leitch from Theologie der Hoffnung, 5th ed., Chr. Kaiser Verlag, Munich, 1965.

Acknowledgment is also gladly given for permission to quote the following sources:

From The Future of Man by Pierre Teilhard de Chardin, copyright © 1959 by Editions du Seuil under the title, L'Avenir de l'Homme; English translation copyright © 1964 by William Collins Sons & Co., Ltd., London, and Harper & Row, Publishers, New York; first Harper Torchbook edition published in 1969. Reprinted by permission of Harper & Row, Publishers, Inc. and William Collins Sons & Co., Ltd.

From Christianity and Evolution by Pierre Teilhard de Chardin, copyright © 1969 by Editions du Seuil; English translation copyright © 1971 by William Collins Sons & Co., Ltd. and Harcourt Brace Jovanovich, Inc. Reprinted by permission of Harcourt Brace Jovanovich, Inc. and William Collins Sons & Co., Ltd.

TABLE OF CONTENTS

PREFACE

St. Paul saw fit to describe Christians simply as people who have hope (Eph. 2:12; 1 Thess. 4:13), and from their earliest days Christians have been admonished to answer for their hope (1 Pet. 3:15). For these reasons, this study undertakes an exploration into the phenomenon of Christian hope, especially as it comes to bear upon the task of ethical reflection. My hypothesis is that the dynamism of Christian hope is meant to serve as both a liberating and a shaping element in the effort to translate the faith-experience of Christians into ethical decisions and activity. To the extent that hope has traditionally been the weak sister of the theological virtues as they impinge upon Christian reflection, it is judged necessary in chapter one of our study to indicate that this investigation into Christian hope is not the result of an arbitrary decision, but springs rather from a definite understanding of the scope and purpose of the human ethical enterprise.

As a critical force within society, ethics must be informed by an imagination which propels us beyond a fascination with the status quo. Human imagination, however, does not develop within a vacuum, but is, in fact, generated and vitalized by our memory; within the context of faith this relationship between imagination and memory comes to mean that there can be no ethics without theology. More specifically, the Christian faith-experience, relating as it does to God's covenantal promise made in the past and pledged to fulfillment in the future, serves both to stimulate and to direct human imagination, for our freedom to move into a new and unknown future is a freedom also to move in a direction indicated at least initially in God's commitment to establish us as his people. Through our exposure to the promised future of God, Christians are inspired to hope. Christian ethics, then, must give expression to our realization that we are an eschatological people and that, as such, we are men and women of hope, whose expectations are well-founded in the faithful promises of a God who calls us to a loving commitment to labor obediently for the appearance of a new age.

In practice, the need for memory and imagination in ethical reflection is seen in contemporary reactions against the inadequacies of purely situational morality. Two examples of the effort to expand the boundaries of the ethical situation are cited in the espousal of a revitalization of the natural-law theory, and in the proposal for an eschatological ethics of promise. These explorations into natural law and eschatology need not be at cross-purposes, but it is my contention that in keeping with the very nature of Christianity, all Christian ethical reflection must be cast finally within the mold of eschatology, which does havoc neither to the nature of humanity nor to our hope for a meaningful history. In an eschatological ethics we are encouraged to explore and develop the possibilities of history, but at the same time an inviolable place is kept for the revolutionary initiative of God.

An attempt is made in chapter two to unveil the characteristics which mark the reality of hope. Here data of the social sciences, philosophy and theology are brought to bear in order to establish in some detail the positive content of references to the phenomenon of hope. On the basis of the data presented from the perspectives both of human and Christian experience, hope reveals itself as an attitude of quiet anticipation that is moved to action by the love which is both its reason for being and the explanation of its communal nature. Psychologically and theologically, it is the availability of help which enables us to hope, and thus to establish a balanced response to the demands of love which calls out for hope to prove itself, now in the action of resistance, now in the action of suffering.

In chapters three and four we pursue our investigation into hope by exploring the specifically theological function which it plays in the thinking of Teilhard de Chardin and Jürgen Moltmann. As different as their theological presuppositions and developments may be, these two men share the conviction that it is hope which, once it is inspired by the knowledge of faith, in turn enlivens faith and succeeds in translating the spirit of Christianity into the needed works of justice and love. For Teilhard, Christ is portrayed primarily as Christ the Evolver, who invites us to labor in co-operation with him for the completion of the redemptive process by incarnating the energy of love in a world-society. Speaking in more biblical terms, Moltmann presents us with a God who inspires hope because his basic self-revelation takes form in a promise to be with us always in a covenantal relationship as we struggle in history to approximate the quality of life that will be fully realized only with the final appearance of God's coming kingdom. Both Teilhard and Moltmann appreciate the fact that as Christians we are both encouraged and guided in our efforts at an ethical existence by the expectation of divine assistance, which allows us to move into the future with hope, but not without exercising a creative responsibility. Liberated, then, by the gospel of God's promise and directed by its commands, we Christians are moved by our hope into a response of what I shall refer to as enduring "expectant creativity."

In the concluding chapter an attempt is made to explain in a more systematic way how hope enlivens the theologies of Teilhard and Moltmann, and thus comes to provide a dynamism by means of which ethical reflection is shaped. It is argued also that the importance and relevancy of an ethics of hope lie precisely in its ability to soothe the present outrage of conscience over the general ineffectualness of religion in the world. The involvement of Christians in the world, and their commitment to laboring for the betterment of humanity, are maintained by means of a dialectical perseverance of faith in the past, hope in the future and love in the present. Such a dialectic indicates that an ethics of Christian hope will be adequate only to the extent that it is able to sustain a methodology of juxtaposition in which both the past and the present, as well as the future, are remembered.

A word must be said, finally, about the nature of this present study. It is at best a prolegomenon to, and a plea for, the concrete business of ethicizing in the mode of Christian hope. Its conviction is that such an enterprise is both rendered possible, and is required, by the structure of Christian theology. This study, however, does not detail the actual shape of Christian life as it gradually gives expression to our decision to act in hope with our neighbors, near and far.

As my work on this book draws to a close, I gladly acknowledge my indebtedness to all those who have had some part in its composition and preparation. Among my teachers, I offer my thanks to James Laney, E. Clinton Gardner and Ted Weber; it was under their proddings that this work found its first shape. I am most grateful to my friend and colleague, Martin R. Tripole, S.J. who kindly agreed to read the manuscript in its final stages and to offer me the benefit of his sensitivity and learning. Finally, I want to express my appreciation to the Director and staff of Saint Joseph's University Press. Mr. Carmen Croce and Patricia Morrissey were immensely helpful in making suggestions regarding the layout of the book, and Catherine McSherry did a masterful job in typing the manuscript. Lest it be forgotten, the virtues and strengths of this book have their origins in many sources; for the work's inadequacies, however, I alone assume responsibility.

xii

CHAPTER I
MEMORY AND IMAGINATION: ESCHATOLOGY'S EXPANSION OF THE LOCUS OF ETHICAL REFLECTION

Introduction

> Go, and catch a falling star,
> Get with child a mandrake root,
> Tell me, where all past years are,
> Or who cleft the Devil's foot . . .[1]

Such is the task that every artist, sculptor, philosopher, or theologian undertakes in the attempt to capture the spirit of any age. There is so much movement and vitality, so much variation in any era, that never can its spirit be imprisoned. Always the spirit of one age takes flight into the next, and every movement becomes but one pathway along which history pushes forward. And yet any meaningful self-expression or human communication rests on affirming, at least implicitly, the possibility of somehow discerning the signs of the times. The recognition of this possibility serves as one reason for the present attempt to enter into the on-going dialogue among theologians concerning the predicament of Christian ethics and their predictions, expectations, and suggestions for the shape of its future.

While the main focus of our discussion in this study will be on the function of Christian hope as a dynamism in ethical reflection and activity, it is the purpose of this first chapter to indicate that this subject is not the result of an arbitrary decision. It springs, rather, from a definite understanding of the overall scope and purpose of the human ethical enterprise, which both in theory and in practice is threatened with its own demise unless it can resist and finally break the bonds of narrow conceptualizations. On the theoretical level we will argue that as a critical analyst of society, ethics must be informed by an imagination which propels it beyond fascination with the status quo. Moreover, just as a productive imagination is nourished by a lively memory, so also does vital ethical reflection have roots in a solid historical tradition. Within a context of faith this hypothesis implies that in order for ethics to be a developer and defender of imagination it must be supported by a viable theology.[2]

1

More specifically, the Christian faith-experience, grounded as it is on God's covenantal promises made in the past and pledged to fulfillment in the future, serves both to stimulate and to direct human imagination. The reason for this is that the freedom to move into a new and unknown future is a freedom also to move in a direction indicated at least initially in our invitation to become God's people. Through our exposure to the promised future of God, Christians are inspired to hope. In embodying this hope, Christian ethics gives expression to the realization that we are eschatological beings whose expectations are well-founded in the faithful promises of a God who calls us to a loving commitment to labor obediently for the appearance of a new age. Thus the Christian's imagination comes to maturity under the influence of the eschatological promises and the fundamental hope to which they inspire us.

In our own time the need for memory and imagination in the ethical enterprise is witnessed in the various attempts by contemporary Christian ethicists to expand the locus of ethical reflection beyond pure situationalism. On one front this effort has taken form in a reshaping of the teleological natural law theory, while on another front a call has gone out for an ethics of promise which is basically an eschatologically oriented ethics. For philosophical and theological reasons the present study suggests that natural law ethics and eschatological ethics should be viewed in the relationship they bear to one another; in as much as these two models of ethical thinking are sensitive to human nature and to our desire for a meaningful history, they both see individuals as historical and dynamic beings whose ability to maintain some transcendence over the present must be explained.

While natural law theory, in resistance to the arbitrariness of either the isolated present moment or written statutes, appears as an appeal to an unwritten law, an eschatological ethics expects human activity to be conducted in the light of a real, yet indefinable future. In both cases, recognition is given to the freedom of the individual as an historical being, but an eschatologically oriented ethics is more open to novelty and the category of the unexpected. An eschatological ethics investigates, existentially and realistically, the possibilities of history, but not without preserving its trust in the revolutionary initiative of God, who invites us to hope for fulfillment in a new future through our dialogical response of creative obedience.

After explaining the link that binds the methodological frameworks of a teleological natural law theory and ethics in an eschatological mode, this chapter concludes with the proposal that in the final analysis every authentic Christian ethic must be shaped by the imprint of eschatological considerations, and thus must be enlivened by a hope which serves as its formal dynamism.

Imagination and the Task of Ethics

Whatever our reservations about the methodological adequacies or ambiguities of recent situational morality, it must be said on its behalf that it has been loathe to throw up its hands in disgust at contemporary man, or to pretend that we are somewhere other than where we really are. As Louis Dupré has pointed out, situationists, with their emphasis on the personal or subjective dimension of human existence, have brought to light an element grossly neglected by traditionally objective forms of morality; the effect of this emphasis on human subjectivity has been, in part, the increased realization "that the moral good is not a pre-existing entity but a value created by the human spirit."[3] We have slowly learned that little progress is made so long as we are guided primarily by the concern to avoid evil—a concern which unfortunately has been the trademark of traditional morality. At the prodding of the situationists we have been encouraged to admit that our present ethical frameworks simply are inadequate, and we have undertaken to set our sights beyond the uncritical observation of precepts.

Insofar as an ethics cannot adequately be developed apart from basic anthropological considerations, some investigation into the make-up of human nature must be conducted in order to bring the nature and meaning of ethical reflection into proper focus. Employing data collected by Rubem Alves in his provocative essay suggesting a program for ethics, we discover that humanity possesses a "condition of possibility," a predisposition, which pushes us beyond complacency with the status quo. Human actions, while conditioned by the past, are never totally delineated by it, and cannot fully be understood apart from our ability to project. To the "ecstatic, projecting dynamism of consciousness" which "indicates that although man is in-the-world, he is not submerged in it," Alves gives the name, imagination; to the extent that one effect of imagination is to see "that things should stop being as they are, in order to become

3

something else," Alves here uncovers a relationship between the role of the imagination and the meaning of the ethical enterprise as it is described by Ernst Cassirer: "The very nature and character of ethical thought is that it can never condescend to accept the 'given.' The ethical world is never given; it is forever in the making."[4] This idea is echoed by Herbert Marcuse who understands that by means of our imagination we begin to exercise our ability to name "the things that are absent" and in this way to break "the spell of the things that are."[5]

If we describe the result of our imaginative involvement in the world as the creation of a utopia in the sense in which this word is used by Cassirer, namely, as a portrait of no actual political or social order, then we can say that an element of the utopian is called for in each of us, and not least of all in the ethician.[6] For Alves, the lack of utopian or imaginative thought is synonymous with the inability to transcend given facts. When this situation prevails, human consciousness relaxes in a state of total conformity with the present world. As a result, failing in imagination, we are unable to be factors in the creation of a new order, because our human reason remains basically operational, a function of the present system or structure of life. We live, then, without perspective, and fail to see either our own life or our relationship to the world as a venturesome undertaking. This means, in turn, that the ethical enterprise is restricted to "problem-solving" within the given structures of life and society; what escapes question is the legitimacy of the structures themselves. This consitutes what Alves calls the domestication of imagination, and it is an especially powerful threat in a technological society which labors under the assumptions that the value questions are already answered, and that the task of establishing a more human society is accomplished simply by know-how.[7] But this domestication is only the first of three threats which can destroy the effectiveness of our imagination. If we are to appreciate fully the importance of imagination's role in life, and if, at the same time, we are to assess the requirements of an adequate methodology for an ethical program, we must now locate briefly the two remaining threats to our imagination.

One of these threats is that imagination may be eclipsed or rendered superfluous, as often occurs among revolutionaries who believe that the given contradictions within a society will lead to a new order if only enough action is inaugurated to intensify the contradictions by opposing the powers which keep the present closed and enslaved. There is a resemblance here to Nietzsche's "slave morality" which arises from resentment and contains no element of affirmation or creativity. Action is really reaction, and eventually it suffers the fate of becoming a reactionary ideology. In the end, no new society is created; the old one simply reappears with the original contradictions inverted.[8]

The final threat confronting imagination is the possibility that at the hands of dreamers and visionaries, it may become "unhooked" from reality, alienated from the real world, ungrounded in such a way that a false world, autonomous in itself, begins to function as a substitute-gratification for the real world. In this instance, instead of continuing the struggle to change the real world, we leave reality as it is and exhaust our human energy in creating new states of consciousness, often idealized, as is evident in many of our sub-cultures. The work of imagination thus becomes a form of spiritual self-indulgence, where effort may be pleasurable but in the end fails to find fulfillment in the fertilization of the real world.[9]

Memory and Theological Ethics

It is in recognizing and resisting these threats that the ethical enterprise finds definition; it seeks the establishment and preservation of imagination's freedom from domestication, from reactionary ideology, and from visionary alienation. Almost immediately, however, a paradoxical ingredient asserts itself, for we discover that human imagination is related to our ability to remember. Our imagination is really only as rich as is our memory. Thus, forgetfulness of the past may well explain the threat of total eclipse which hangs over imagination, and against which ethics must labor. This link between memory and imagination lies at the root, perhaps, of Marcuse's statement that "remembrance of the past may give rise to dangerous insights, and the established society seems to be apprehensive to the subversive contents of memory."[10] There is a terrifying poignancy in the realization that if we succeed in inducing amnesia in someone, that person's future comes under our control, and thereby we have mastered the technique for the suppression of human freedom.[11] This is an hypothesis which goes a long way in explaining both the secret of the nearly four-hundred-year-old frustration of slavery endured by the Black People of America, and the critical function served by such phenomena as the emphases on "Black History," "Black Culture," and "African Studies."

It is our memory that generates and vitalizes human imagination, and in this way transforms us into utopian beings. Moreover, Alves is right in saying that within the context of faith this relationship between memory and imagination comes to mean that there can be no ethics without theology, for theological language, whatever else its foundation, is based on memory. Nowhere, perhaps, is this more clearly seen than in the language of Christian faith which tells both of the redemptive liberation of the human race in history, and of the way in which this liberation must continue to be won.[12] It is important to realize that as Christians our memory's role is not exhausted solely in recalling the events of the past. For our past is peculiar; it continually re-creates us in such a way as to make the most of our present, and it enlivens us so as to attend to the future promised us by God. Recalling our past serves to remind us of the richness of the present which is the future in the making, while at the same time we are encouraged to remember in hope the future we are already gifted with by God's promise.

The Christian faith-experience, relating as it does to covenantal promises made in the past and pledged to fulfillment in the future, serves both to stimulate and to shape imagination. By being directed toward the future, Christians are motivated to resist the forces of domestication and ideology, while at the same time, through the urgings of our historical memory, we are restrained in our imaginings from submitting to the lure of alienation and ineffectualness. As Christians, we remember that our imagination is to serve us in the struggle to continue the liberating transformation of the world.

As a response to what love has already done for us, and as an anticipation of what love is yet to accomplish, Christianity presents itself as a liberated movement into the future, but it experiences its freedom precisely because of, and by means of, its definite historical boundaries as these emerge in light of the real eschatological promises which are remembered in faith. Moreover, the freedom to move into a new and unknown future is a freedom really to move with imagination and hope in a direction indicated, at least initially, in the covenantal promises of God.

Thus, within the context of faith, the anticipation and imagination of the future is more than mere wish-determined thought; it is the expectation of the fulfillment of what has already begun. The Christian uses the eschatological promises as a constant critique of any status quo, something which is possible only because of the transcendent nature of these promises. In this way we resist the domestication of our imagination whereby it is reduced to a functionary role in service to a social, or political, or even theological system. At the same time, in response to the other threats against imagination, it may be safely said that Christian action is not totally explained simply as a denial or negation of the present. Rather the overriding impetus of Christian life takes its meaning from the positive struggle to co-operate in the establishment of the future of God. Finally, the dangers of alienation—of fantasizing, of submitting to an illusion, of pure wish ful-thinking, and of irresponsible escapism —are obviated in the constant remembrance of the promises of God and of the conditions of our fidelity.

Nor may we conclude, as some have done, that the historical roots of Christian faith work only to curtail the possibility of a truly new future. Thus a reminder is in order, namely, that the content of the new future is described in only the broadest terms of peace, justice, truth, love, and liberation from suffering and oppression; not even the details of how we are to co-operate in the building of the future are spelled out. Our faith-inspired memory gifts us only with the sensitivity to discern the Spirit and to follow where He leads. As Alves puts it, the community of faith possesses "the insight necessary to distinguish between the groaning of the Spirit, as He expresses Himself throughout the world, and the snoring of domesticated men."[13] In the final analysis, then, ethics is concerned with bringing a vital imagination to bear upon the creation of a new world. To do this, Christian ethics reminds us that we are an eschatological people and that, as such, we are called to the exercise of an imagination and a hope whose expectations are well-founded in the faithful promises of a God who urges us to make a loving commitment in laboring for the appearance of a new age.

Reshaping the Ethical Context

So far we have argued for the appearance of an ethics whose methodology arises out of a perduring relationship between memory and imagination. We must now ask if there is any correspondence between this proposal and the way in which Christian ethical reflection has been developing recently. One point must be made clear. Among Christian ethicists we may find few specific references to human imagination as such, and yet an appreciation of its role in ethical reflection may be implicit, for, in truth, the imagination need not be viewed as a special isolated faculty. Rather, as William Lynch has noted, imagination "is all the faculties, all the resources, all the history of man, brought to bear upon the concrete world of man, outside and inside of man, in order that he may form such images of the world as will help him to live and breathe in that world." Thus, the activity of imagination reveals itself in the struggle "to reach into existence itself" and there to find or to make a world which is not yet but which shall be, a world of the future, of the possible.[14] In this vein, then, my contention is that the only methodology adequate to the demands of a Christian ethics is one which seriously acknowledges the fact that humanity must broaden and deepen its dominion over time: over the past by means of historical knowledge, over the present by accurate and realistic analysis, and over the future by the art of imaginative projecting and planning.

With this proposition in mind, and despite the danger of over-simplification, it may be stated fairly that many criticisms leveled against the various forms of purely situational morality have been shaped by the general recognition that the ethical situation has been too narrowly defined, in terms both of space and of time. Thus, in addition to their reluctance to consider a person's communal or societal involvements in any expansive way when it comes to rendering moral decisions, many situationists have come either to fear or to forget the past; no less, however, have they often closed their eyes to the future. Reactions against situationalism's tendency to establish too arbitrary a definition of the ethical situation have taken two interesting and provocative forms. One is the development of a revisionist natural law theory and the other is a proposal for an eschatological ethic of promise. The attempt in the work of both the natural law revisionist and the advocate of eschatological ethics is to illuminate any present human situation as a locus for ethical reflection by viewing that situation in as complete a way as possible, precisely by evaluating it in terms of its relationship to a past, a future and a more expansive present. Although we are concerned in this study with how the dynamism of eschatological hope formally serves as a liberating and shaping element in the Christian's endeavor at ethical reflection, at least a few words must be said here about how the context of ethical decision-making is expanded by some present-day emphases on natural law theory.

8

As a concrete expression of how a revisionist natural law theory serves to extend the boundaries of any ethical situation, Herbert McCabe suggests that recourse to the theory of natural law is essentially an attempt to identify and highlight the primary situation in which any person finds himself, the situation, that is, whose demands take priority over the demands of any and all other situations. A person's primary situation is, of course, his relationship to humanity as a whole.[15] To illustrate his point, McCabe presents an example from the animal kingdom as described by Konrad Lorenz, to the effect that when two wolves are fighting, if one "submits" by offering his unprotected throat in a ritual gesture to his opponent and conqueror, he will not be killed. McCabe comments that the victorious wolf acts in accordance with an innate inhibition against killing another wolf and thereby threatening the species. In thus refraining from killing, the wolf is not submitting to some exterior force, but rather to a depth within himself. Deep-down, the wolf does not want to kill a member of his species. We see here a struggle between two levels of wanting: on one level the wolf is stimulated by the immediate circumstances of the fight with its anger and excitement, while on another, deeper, level he is necessitated by the long-range needs of the wolf-species as a whole.

In an analogous way, we as human beings experience various levels of wanting, and McCabe suggests that when we obey the natural law, the law of our species, we are being true to a depth within ourselves, whereas when we act contrary to this law we violate ourselves at the center of our being, and at the same time we forget the prior demands of our primary and comprehensive human situation.[16] In presenting his reflections on natural law, McCabe draws upon parallel thoughts of D. H. Lawrence:

> All that matters is that men and women should do what they really want to do. Though here as elsewhere [he is discussing sex and marriage] we must remember that man has a double set of desires, the shallow and the profound, the personal, superficial, temporary desires, and the inner, impersonal, great desires that are fulfilled in long periods of time. The desires of the moment are easy to recognize, but the others, the deeper ones, are difficult. It is the business of our Chief Thinkers to tell us of our deeper desires, not to keep shrilling our little desires into our ears. . . . .

. . . . Man has little needs and deeper needs. We have fallen into the mistake of living from our little needs till we have almost lost our deeper needs in a sort of madness. There is a little morality which concerns persons and the little needs of man; and this, alas, is the morality we live by. But there is a deeper morality, which concerns all womanhood, all manhood, and nations and races and classes of men. This greater morality affects the destiny of mankind over long stretches of time, applies to man's greater needs and is often in conflict with the little morality of the little needs.[17]

The advantage of such an understanding of the natural law and of its function is that it indicates that the adequacy of ethical decision-making demands that in practice morality be more than an attempt to respond sensitively to the details of the here-and-now. Or perhaps we may more accurately say that the natural law theory reminds us that we cannot in fact adequately understand the present moment nor perceive its ethical imperative unless that moment is illuminated by the highlights cast upon it by its place in a broader spatial-temporal context.

In turning to an example of how ethics in an eschatological context reacts to situational morality, the work of Vernard Eller is helpful. Eller argues for what he calls an "ethic of promise" in which the kingdom principle—"which action will be of greater service to the kingdom?"—is used as the guideline in making ethical decisions.[18] He describes the eschatological ethics of promise as being contextualist, absolutist, perfectionist, heroic, tension-producing and, finally and essentially, an arcane discipline. The overall effect of Eller's proposal is to open up the ethical situation in such a way that every action is evaluated and every decision is made in light of its relationship "to the overarching purpose and goal of history, which is the coming kingdom of God." The "context" of present actions must include more than simply the present, for the present is actually God's future in the process of becoming and ethical decisions must, therefore, be oriented to that future. The fact that the absolute, or the norm of perfection, is seen within this context, not as a code which was decreed in the past, but as a promise of what shall be in the future, demands of Christians that they continually and heroically resist the temptation to acquiesce in the status quo. Because they march to a different drummer, Christians necessarily are involved in an "arcane discipline."[19] What they do is seen by others as somewhat strange or unusual.

The reason for this, says Eller, is that "an ethical system based upon a promise that the people have not heard, calling men to venture toward a reality they do not see, will never make sense and cannot be expected to make sense to a secular world." The ethics of promise, then, is an "arcane discipline" which is at one and the same time a demand and a source of strength "hidden from the eyes of the world precisely because it is a secret wrapped in the gospel promise not yet accepted by the world."[20] Christians are precisely those who act upon God's promise; they act as though that promise were coming true, and in such a way as to allow it to come true.[21] As people who act with hope in a future whose fulfillment is promised, but to whose attainment they must attend, Christians are eschatological beings, and of necessity their ethical decisions must reflect their orientation toward the future promised them.

On the basis of the future which is expected in light of remembered promises, Christian consciousness discovers in and through the present a continuity between past and future. For this reason, it can mediate between radical futurists who explicitly reject any continuity with the past and thus call for a total revolution, and traditionalists who resist all progress and move through history with their backs to the future.[22] And yet, we must insist that the expected future is not simply an evolution from the past; the element of discontinuity is introduced into the process of history insofar as the very foundation of the process is marked precisely by the category of "promise," and "promise" as such "does not illuminate existing reality; rather, it contradicts it."[23] Since the category of "promise" contains within itself the elements of "gift," of gratuity and unexpectedness, history, as a pathway into the future, is for the believer, in addition to being more than a development of the past, also more than a memory or repetition of the past. And yet, while Christians look to real newness in the future, their ability to do so, as well as their direction and momentum, take shape undeniably from the past.[24]

Eschatological Existence and Theological Ethics

Aware of the inevitable historicity of human existence, we are called to reflect upon the status of our moral activity in terms of the whole temporal continuum. While the past has been amply praised for its contribution to the human understanding of the present, and while the present is rightly appreciated as the building-block of the future, we are only now beginning to see the influence that a vision of the future may have upon our involvements in the here and now, and upon our determination to mold our present environment as we see fit. Because the individual is not only a partic-ipator in the "already here," but also a creator of the "not yet," we must be concerned ineluctably with our responsibility for the consequences, present and future, of our activity.

Such an enterprise in no way implies the arbitrariness of sheer relativism for there is, indeed, "a constant direction implicit in the notion of a dynamically conceived morality." It is the movement toward "fuller humanity."[25] This formal idea of "fuller humanity" needs to be given content, but at this point it may be said that all morality is humanistic in that it promises its adherents the most authentic human existence. Some continuity between the Judeo-Christian tradition and other modes of ethical reflection may be seen to lie in the pursuit of this common goal of "fuller humanity;" nonetheless, an undeniable element of discontinuity arises in the fact that for many outside the Judeo-Christian tradition, the attainment of such a goal is teleological in that human transcendence means simply the attainment of an authenticity that is reached self-sufficiently as the full flowering of the individual's innate possibilities or potentialities; for Christians, however, authentic humanity is more eschatological, which is to say that it involves the acknowledgment of a gift, and requires and demands the free acceptance of that gift. What inspires Christians is not so much the goal of becoming divine through human effort, but rather the goal of becoming human with the help of, and in co-operation with, God who approaches individ-uals and invites them to come closer.[26]

Since human beings are unavoidably situated in the world, "fuller humanity," as the goal of morality, immediately acquires some content for it is seen as necessarily involving "care for bodily existence and an affirmative relation to the world."[27] Theologically, this attitude toward the world is aligned with a serious regard for the Incarnation, understood as God's total immersion into matter in order to effect complete redemption. It is faith in, and hope for, the full redemption of people and their world which create the pressure behind responsible Christian service. Moreover, active social and political concern proves the truth of the Christian's belief in the coming redemption of the body, for the expectation of the resurrection obliges us to an operative involvement with humanity's physical future. At one and the same time, Christians must be committed to personal intervention in the movement of history while remaining always open to God's gift of the future, thereby refusing to separate their hope for God's kingdom and their hope for this world.[28]

In the realm of ethics this means that the believer must be concerned with penultimates as well as with ultimates, in an attitude, not simply of withdrawal and worldly renunciation, but of right use and enjoyment of the things of the world. And yet, our being-in-the-world must be kept in tension with our being-on-the-way. In this dialectic, we must manifest a responsibility which leaves no doubt of the fact that while we do not submit to an externally imposed authoritarian code, we are, nevertheless, answerable or accountable to a transcendence which lays unconditional claim upon us. Here both secularists and Christians come close in recognizing the fact that they "have a small part in the total venture of creation." But a difference remains in that, as Roger Shinn has suggested, the secularist is committed to a closed humanism in which humanity is the measure and judge of all things, whereas the Christian, as one who co-operates with God in the stewardship of the world, is involved in an open humanism.[29]

In their struggle toward the realization of authentic human existence for themselves and others, Christians bear witness to the function which utopian considerations fulfill in inspiring creative and imaginative involvements in the present. Christians indeed know eminently well that just as the future takes shape under the influence of the present, so also are their decisions about the present shaped by their vision of the future. In light of the eschatological promises, Christians realize that human existence has a profound dimension which prescribes a mode of action, one that expresses and incarnates a way of being, namely, that of hoping, such that we are to act in accordance with "whom-we-hope-to-be." "Who-we-hope-to-be" is part of our being, our nature. Our human hopes are shaped by the very conditions of possibility with which we were gifted in our creation by God, and these conditions of possibility were verified and renewed in the redemptive covenant revealed in Jesus Christ. For this

13

reason, we understand that we cannot achieve authentic humanity if we prescind from "whom-we-hope-to-be." "Who-we-hope-to-be" in light of God's covenantal promises shapes our present mode of being and must be reflected in our ethical decisions and activity.

As Christians we are grateful for the real possibilities for human development which we enjoy; at the same time, we appreciate that the exploration and development of these possibilities cannot be arbitrary and haphazard. Our past establishes our present, and our future exists because of a promise which led us out of an Egypt where we were secure in a closed system of morality. Now we are involved in an Exodus where the natural or human order is invaded by more than immanent requirements. Human action must open itself to be molded in response to the action of God who loves us with an ever-lasting love. Our lives must, in short, be lived expressions of what Paul Ramsey has described as "a morality of the Exodus."[30] We must live as an eschatological people, a people of hope.

I regard hope as a basic constituent of the dynamism needed to achieve, realize, and complete the potential both of human and of Christian existence. I am not suggesting that this is the sole factor, because hope is a quality of human existence and as such does not ever function in an isolated form. As one of the traditionally-cited theological virtues, it operates in conjunction with the qualities of faith and charity so that if faith is real, a necessary result will be evidenced in the display of hope. But if faith is false without hope, so also is hope impossible without faith. Faith also is a grounding of love; it facilitates love when the latter is humanly difficult. Hope, at the same time, frees us from anxiety and fear so that today we may love more effectively and thereby hasten the appearance of the new future. In short, as Jürgen Moltmann suggests, hope manifests itself in the life of the Christian as a believing hope, where faith has the priority, but hope the primacy:

> Without faith's knowledge of Christ, hope becomes a utopia and remains hanging in the air. But without hope, faith falls to pieces, becomes a fainthearted and ultimately a dead faith. It is through faith that man finds the path of true life, but it is only hope that keeps him on that path. Thus it is that faith in Christ gives hope its assurance. Thus it is that hope gives faith in Christ its breadth and leads it into life.[31]

We will return in the next chapter to a consideration of hope's relationship to faith and love. For now, let us say simply that in Christian consciousness, the past is assimilated by a **faithful** memory allowing the revealed eschatological promises to shape our understanding and evaluation of the present situation. At the same time, in **hopeful** anticipation and planning for the future fulfillment of the promises, the Christian is impelled here and now to a **loving** critique and reconstruction of those personal and social elements in human existence which thwart the development of the kingdom of God. The eschatological promises establish the truest and fullest context of Christian experience, and only in light of the hope which is inspired by these promises—a hope belonging more to the order of "being" than to that of "having"—does Christian ethics receive direction and a quality of control which strikes a balance between Revivalism's detached and ineffectual hope for a coming kingdom, and Liberalism's humanistic desire for the progressive transformation of this world into heaven on earth.

The eschatological mode of ethical reflection as suggested by a theology of hope rests on the image of the individual as a responsible agent, but it also incorporates within itself elements of both deontology and teleology. Thus a person is called both to respond in faithful obedience to the conditions of the eschatological promises, and at the same time to pursue an ideal good with an appropriate appreciation of the contribution which his or her personal action makes to the fulfillment of the world. In an eschatologically conceived ethics, however, the model of responsibility is highlighted in the fact that God's action through the initiative of grace remains foremost and central.

The future is as much one which is coming to us as one toward which we move on our own. Nevertheless, move we must, and in an atmosphere of hope, which is not an optimism based simply on human achievement or on the ideal of evolutionary progress. Neither is our eschatological hope fulfilled automatically, but only in relationship to our laboring in and with anticipation of its realization. There is always a dialectic of grace and endeavor, but also always the possibility of an opening to a new future, always the "possibility that grace will transmute folly and death into atonement and resurrection" so that finally the human condition is something incomprehensible in merely human terms. [32] As an eschatological being, the Christian may never enjoy the leisure of passive detachment.

On the contrary, just as secular revolutions have their seeds, not in despair, but in frustrated or curtailed hopes, hopes that are too long in being fulfilled, so also are Christian conversion and commitment embodied in a social responsibility which is shaped in light of the hope inspired by the eschatological promises of a new future. In acknowledgment of the fundamental dignity enjoyed by people even now, Christians are moved to action, but to action moderated by the expectations placed upon them by the covenantal promises of God.

Eschatological existence, then, has to do, finally, with the perspective in which we view the future. It offers a third possibility to the alternatives which say that we must choose "between gradual progress, a steady ascent towards the last day, and a catastrophic break in history." For the Christian, the parousia, the new future, comes indeed at the culmination of human efforts to transform the world, but it comes also as the last in a series of revolutions, rather than as the final term of evolution. As is characteristic of all revolutionary advances, the Christian future contains an element of the new and unexpected, but there is also a continuity which becomes evident only in retrospect.[33]

This last point has been developed in an essay by Harvey Cox on the need for a new perspective concerning the relationship between tradition and the future.[34] Cox suggests that of the three ways of perceiving the future—the apocalyptic, the teleological, and the prophetic—only the last proves adequate for effective ethical involvement in the present. This prophetic perspective, which is the characteristically Hebraic view, presents the future "as an open field of human hope and responsibility." This is the perspective employed by the prophets who "recalled Yahweh's promise as a way of calling the Israelites into moral action in the present." Except for the assurance "that Yahweh, who has promised to persevere with his people, will not abandon them," the future is not predetermined. From this prophetic, or what we have been calling eschatological, perspective, human beings appear as dynamic beings who use history as an arena for responsible freedom where the past is recalled to memory, not that it may be divinized, but in order to keep in mind that the God of the covenant still expects things from his people in the future. In developing its understanding of humanity, prophetic eschatology focuses upon a crucial dimension of our existence— our "answerability for the future."

16

Our search for an adequate framework for Christian ethical reflection leads us to the perspective which "produces both the terror and the joy inherent in the recognition that the future will be what man will make of it." At the same time, however, central to this perspective is the realization that although we can and must shape the future, it is not ours in the end to bring history to a close. All human ethical and political endeavors must be informed, therefore, "by a bold provisionality" which "frees us from having to build for eternity or solve things once and for all."[35] Because, on the one hand, there is no human "final solution" for anything, and because, on the other hand, historical responsibility is expected in light both of God's promise and of its demands for human involvement, it follows for the Christian that the proper ethical stance must embrace both hopeful waiting and active planning for the future; the Christian's life is one of human co-operation with the divine initiative. There is room for brave and revolutionary advances into the future with its newness and unexpectedness, but there is also a call to moderation in that the final transformation of history is completed by God, who himself establishes and, in the end, reveals the basic continuity of human existence.

An eschatological ethic, recognizing, as it does, the initiative manifested by God's perduring and operative presence in past, present, and future history, portrays human activity as free, but undeniably responsive. The norm of human action appears in who we already are in view of, and even on the basis of, who we are to become. In other words, the "becoming," the future element of human existence, is already influential in our present decision-making processes. In light of the eschatological promises embodied in God's covenantal relationship with his people, we have come to expect a new future, a future not entirely of our making, but one for whose appearance, according to the very terms of the covenant, we bear a definite responsibility. As eschatological beings, then, Christians, while full of hope and intent upon a fuller humanity in the future, remember in faith that their existence is informed even now by God who calls them to covenantal fidelity through present commitments of love.

Summary

The time has come to get our bearings. We began with a consideration of Alves' proposal that in view of human existence as transcendence of the present, the whole ethical enterprise must itself be concerned with preserving and guaranteeing a liberated imagination such that we do not fall vicitm to technological domestication, to revolutionary ideology, or to futile visionary alienation. To insure that the necessary utopian function of human imagination remains vital and productive demands, however, that we be solidly rooted in a meaningful past and present through the workings of a reliable and comprehending memory. We have here a theoretical and rather skeletal framework upon which to envision the emerging shape of Christian ethics. It is a theory which claims that by its very essence ethical reflection must exceed and transcend the confines of the present moment or situation through the use of memory and imagination.

This need to extend the boundaries of the ethical situation is recognized by various Christian ethicians in their respective reactions to the narrowness of purely situational morality. Thus, McCabe has issued a call to reconsider natural law theory and its function in establishing the common bonds and deep roots of all humanity, with the idea in mind that only in this way is it possible to uncover and evaluate the complex dimensions of moral existence. A different approach has been suggested by Eller in his proposal of an eschatological ethics of promise, which takes seriously the present demands initiated by the real power of the future kingdom of God.

In synthesizing these perspectives my suggestion is that an adequate methodology for Christian ethics must take serious account of the human desire and capacity to have dominion over time. This desire is really an expression of our need to be at one with ourselves, both through a meaningful assimilation of our past by means of historical knowledge, and through a fruitful anticipation of our future using a dialectic of imaginative hoping and planning. In recognition of this human need, natural law with its teleology encompasses human history, past, present and future, by exposing the underlying conditions of possibility which explain our present existence and indicate our potentiality for future development. But to this requirement for an adequate Christian ethics another stipulation must be added, namely, that Christian ethics must acknowledge that in our relationship to time, in our quest to shape and move history, we are not totally autonomous and self-sufficient beings. Rather, Christians direct their history into a new future that is already promised them. It is a future achieved in Christ Jesus, but it is also a future not yet completed. Finally, it is a future which opens up possibilities and liberates humanity to hope, but it is also a future which demands that we explore these possibilities within the general contours laid out in the eschatological promises of God.

We may say, then, that both natural-law ethics and eschatological modes of ethical reflection rest on a view of persons which sees them in search of a fuller humanity. This is a philosophical anthropology which is phenomenologically sound. And yet, insofar as this search implies a constant and conscious development—in one instance, evolutionary, and in the other, more revolutionary—we must ask for an explanation of the continuing motivation and impetus behind this human struggle for fulfillment. In this regard, it has been suggested by Teilhard de Chardin that once evolution has reached the stage of reflective consciousness, continuation of the process is the result of a decision, and even of a vision, that the way to fulfillment is open and accessible.[36]

It appears, then, that in some way hope must lie at the basis of the human movement through history and life, whether this movement be interpreted in the final analysis simply as natural law teleology or, as it is argued here in keeping with the demands of Christianity, as eschatological. In explanation of the persistence of our movement, our historical dynamism, throughout the flux of time, it can only be said that we are creatures of hope. In the following chapters it is precisely as the dynamism of human and Christian existence that the phenomenon of hope will receive our attention, first in its anthropological dimensions, and then in its theological dimensions as a vital element in Christian ethical reflection.

CHAPTER I

REFERENCES

1. The first four lines of John Donne's poem, Song.

2. These suggestions were offered by Rubem Alves, "Some Thoughts on a Program for Ethics," Union Seminary Quarterly Review, XXVI, No. 2 (Winter, 1971), pp. 153-70.

3. Louis Dupré, "The Existentialist Connection of Situation Ethics," The Future of Ethics and Moral Theology, eds. Don Brezine and James V. McGlynn (Chicago: Argus Communications, 1968), pp. 106-13.

4. Alves, "Program for Ethics," p. 159; also see Ernest Cassirer, An Essay on Man (Garden City, N.Y.: Doubleday, 1953), p. 85.

5. Herbert Marcuse, One Dimensional Man (Boston: Beacon Press, 1966), p. 68.

6. Cassirer, Essay on Man, p. 85.

7. Alves, "Program for Ethics," pp. 161-63. This idea and the two remaining threats to human imagination bear remarkable similarity to ideas presented by Erich Fromm in The Revolution of Hope. Toward a Humanized Technology (New York: Bantam Books, 1968), pp. 6-9.

8. Ibid., pp. 163-64. In reference to Nietzsche see Walter Kaufmann, The Portable Nietzsche (New York: Viking Press, 1965), p. 451.

9. Ibid., pp. 164-65.

10. Marcuse, One Dimensional Man, p. 98.

11. Alves, "Program for Ethics," p. 166.

12. Ibid., pp. 166-67.

13. Ibid., p. 167.

14. William F. Lynch, S.J., "Images of Faith," Continuum, 7 (1969-70), 187-94 at 189-90.

15. Herbert McCabe, What Is Ethics All About? (Washington: Corpus Books, 1969), p. 34.

16. Ibid., p. 45 with reference to Konrad Lorenz, King Solomon's Ring (London, 1954), p. 188.

17. Ibid., pp. 60-2 with reference to D. H. Lawrence, Apropos of Lady Chatterly's Lover (London, 1931), pp. 52-3, 80.

18. Vernard Eller, The Promise: Ethics in the Kingdom of God (Garden City, N.Y.: Doubleday, 1970), p. 11.

19. Ibid. pp. 1-6.

20. Ibid., p. 6.

21. Ibid., p.8.

22. Frederick E. Crow, S.J., "Pull of the Future and Link with the Past: On the Need for Theological Method," Continuum, 7 (1969-70), 30-49 at 31.

23. Ibid., p. 36. Also see Jürgen Moltmann, Theology of Hope, trans. James W. Leitch (New York: Harper & Row, 1967), p. 86.

24. Ibid., p. 38.

25. John Macquarrie, Three Issues in Ethics (New York: Harper & Row, 1970), p. 52.

26. Rubem Alves, A Theology of Human Hope (Washington: Corpus Books, 1969), pp. 85-100, where the distinction is drawn between humanistic messianism and messianic humanism.

27. Macquarrie, Three Issues, pp. 53-6.

28. Gerald G. O'Collins, S.J., Man and His New Hopes (New York: Herder & Herder, 1969), pp. 132-133.

29. Macquarrie, Three Issues, pp. 72-7; Roger Shinn, Man: The New Humanism, Vol. 6 of New Directions in Theology Today (Phila.: Westminster Press, 1968), pp. 170-74.

30. Paul Ramsey, "Jacques Maritain and Edmund Cahn: The Egypt of the Natural Law," Nine Modern Moralists (Englewood Cliffs, N.J.: Prentice Hall, 1962), pp. 209-32 at 231-32.

31. Moltmann, Theology of Hope, p. 20.

32. Macquarrie, Three Issues, pp. 143-44.

33. McCabe, What is Ethics?, p. 160; see also "Pastoral Constitution on the Church in the Modern World," No. 39, The Documents of Vatican II, ed. Walter M. Abbott, S.J., trans. ed. Joseph Gallagher (New York: America Press, 1966), p. 237.

34. Harvey Cox, On Not Leaving It To The Snake (New York: Macmillan Paperbacks, 1969), pp. 29-43.

35. Ibid., pp. 34, 39-43.

36. Pierre Teilhard de Chardin, The Phenomenon of Man, trans. Bernard Wall (New York: Harper & Row Torchbooks, 1965), pp. 231-32.

CHAPTER II
THE PHENOMENON OF CHRISTIAN HOPE:
AN ANTHROPOLOGY AND APOLOGIA

Introduction

In the preceding chapter the ethical enterprise was seen as calling for the liberation of human consciousness. It was further suggested that both the fulfillment of the ethical enterprise and the achievement of liberation demand recognition of the human desire and capacity to gain dominion over time—past, present, and future—by assimilation of the past, analysis of the present, and creation of the future. Within the context of Christian faith this means that both our own historical dynamism and the liberation of human consciousness, understood as dominion over time and as the imaginative shaping of history, draw strength from, and are embodied in, an eschatological hope. The basic anthropological and faith components of this hope will concern us in this chapter.

Our intention is to offer first an analysis of the cultural situation of hope, and then to view it from within the perspective of the faith-commitment of Christianity. In the course of our discussion we want to discover the conditions of possibility for an anthropology of hope, an anthropology which serves at the same time as an apologia for the Christian phenomenon of eschatological hope. Hope, indeed, is one of those realities common to the interest of many professions, yet proper to none. It is an object of concern to philosophers, theologians, poets, psychologists, psychiatrists, politicians—and gamblers. In an effort to offer a representative and comprehensive view of hope, we will draw on the data of the social sciences and philosophy. With that background, we will cross over to the threshold of a theological anthropology where we must confront questions about the reasonableness of our hope, and about its relationship to faith. Only then, in following chapters, will we turn our attention to a more detailed examination of the role of hope in ethical reflection as it has evolved in the theologies of Teilhard de Chardin and Jürgen Moltmann.

The Character of Hope

In order to begin where the problematic surrounding hope is perhaps most concretely expressed for an industrialized society, we will examine Erich Fromm's thesis that today's revolution of hope entails the push toward a humanized technology. In order to achieve a generally efficient economic system, America has paid a high price indeed. Not only is she involved in an endless process of manufacturing products which threaten herself and all humanity with physical destruction, but in addition to this the average American has turned into a totally passive consumer whose needs are dictated by the most successful advertising monopoly ever devised. Under the bureaucratic workings of government and big business, the individual is burdened with feelings of frustration and impotence. For Fromm, this raises the question:

> Are we confronted with a tragic, insoluble dilemma? **Must we produce sick people in order to have a healthy economy, or can we use our material resources, our inventions, our computers to serve the ends of man? Must individuals be passive and dependent in order to have strong and well-functioning organizations?**[1]

There is a way out of the dilemma. In fact, there are three possibilities: the way of surrender, the way of revolution, and the way of creative humanization. To surrender is simply to continue in the direction we have taken, recognizing, however, that the likely outcome of this choice is either "thermonuclear war or severe human pathology." To choose the way of revolution is to attempt to change our direction by force, and here the risk is that all further movement may thereby be rendered impossible or meaningless. Fromm himself inclines toward the third possibility, that of humanizing the technological system such that it will contribute to the growth and well-being of the world's people.[2]

It is Fromm's contention that the possibilities of restoring the social system to human control, of activating the individual, and thus of humanizing technology, are grounded in what he sees as an individual's deep longing for life and for new attitudes instead of ready-made schemes and plans. Moreover, the realization of these possibilities can be expected because "the threat to life is today a threat not to one class, to one nation, but a threat to all."[3] And yet, we cannot afford to be naive in our expectations. There is evidence of a widespread hopelessness in America with regard to the possibility of changing the direction in which we are moving. It is a hopelessness all the more difficult to cope with because it is largely unconscious, rooted in people who are consciously "optimistic" and who expect to enjoy the promised generation of "progress."

The first steps toward discovering the real meaning of hope demand an acquaintance with the imitations of hope as they appear in the disguises taken on by human hopelessness. Among the many masks of which hopelessness is fond, two are particularly noteworthy because of the intense contradiction in which they stand against each other. At one extreme what tries to pass as hope is inactivity and passive waiting, while at the opposite extreme a pretense of hope appears in the form of phrase-making and adventurism, where reality is disregarded and an effort is made to force what cannot be forced.

Hope, then, cannot be identified, on the one hand, as the sterile longing for a state of greater vitality or as the desire for relief from boredom. And yet, the exclusion of this kind of longing from the realm of real hope cannot be absolute and outright. It is more accurate, rather, simply to issue the warning that if human expectation is marked by the quality of passiveness it becomes only a cloak for resignation, a mere ideology, and even idolatry in which the enthroned gods and goddesses are "Future," "History," and "Posterity." The attitude here, as Fromm notes, is that "nothing is expected to happen in the **now** but only in the next moment, the next day, the next year, and in another world if it is too absurd to believe that hope can be realized in this world." In more modern bourgeois language, the worship of the future or of history becomes the worship of progress; whatever its terminology, however, the point is, that such a mentality constitutes a threat to human imagination and consequently results in an alienation of the human capacity to create and thus to hope. "Instead of something I do or I become, the idols, future and posterity, bring about something without my doing anything."[4]

On the other hand, just as inimical to true hope is the naive spirit of adventurism with its passion for activity. Through their strategy of contempt for those who do not prefer death to defeat, no matter what the circumstances, it is often possible for false prophets and messiahs to inspire many, especially among the young, to shame and confusion. The result is the spread of hopelessness and nihilism under the guise of a pseudo-radicalism which, for all its boldness and sense of dedication, remains unconvincing because it is marred by a lack of realism, a poor sense of strategy, and little evidence, either of a love for life, or of joy in living.[5]

We should point out here that both Fromm's insistence upon the human ability to master technology and his description of the two most extreme disguises taken on by hopelessness reveal a striking relationship to Alves' warning, referred to in the previous chapter, about the three dangers which threaten human imagination, namely, technological domestication, visionary alienation, and revolutionary ideology. This leads us to suggest that, in one form or another, the basic threat to the maintenance and development of human imagination, and thus to the success of the ethical task, is in fact hopelessness. To counteract the power of hopelessness and its deceits, we must probe more deeply into the experience of hope.

Phenomenologically, hope is a way of transcending the present moment, of moving through present difficulties, and of continually deciding to move into the future. In this light, hope joins hands with human imagination, at least as the latter has been portrayed by William Lynch in his classic work on imagination as healer of the hopeless. Lynch sees human imagination as "the gift that constantly proposes to itself that the boundaries of the possible are wider than they seem." As a result, imagination refuses to be "overcome by the absoluteness of the present moment." Thus the present is relativized by a hopeful imagination, and in fact hope becomes steadier and more mature precisely insofar as it develops the ability to live contextually, in this sense, at least, that it recognizes that things and events "have contexts and are not absolute, atomic units." This relationship between hope and the ability to see things in perspective is well illustrated by the difference in attitude and reaction between a child and a more mature person. A child's absorption in the joys and pains of the present moment is often so total that all hope rises or falls with that instant, while a more mature person is able to endure present frustration because of a hope arising out of a perspective encompassing greater periods of time, both past and future. We can hope because the present is not absolute, and because the way to the future is open. This does not make present suffering any less real;

26

it simply renders it less desperate in that we are no longer totally preoccupied with the present as though it were the whole of reality. It is in this sense that we may speak of transcending the present without, however, any connotation of denying the pain and difficulty of the moment.[6]

There are many suspicions still surrounding the idea of transcendence, but this does not alter the fact that we do indeed possess the ability to endure the present, perdure through it, traverse it, use and shape it, and finally to transgress it—all because of the fact that under the light of a realistic imagination, an imagination which imagines the real, we can locate an event within a context whose dimensions exceed the clear and definite confines of the temporally-present reality. Gabriel Marcel, that master of hope, does not hesitate, in fact, to declare that "what is specific in hope is lost sight of if the attempt is made to judge and condemn it from the point of view of **established experience.**"[7] Thus, hope, by its very nature, imagines what has not yet come to pass, but still is possible; and yet, at the same time the realistic imagination distinguishes itself from the unreal absorptions of daydreams and fantasies "whose object is transient and solitary self-aggrandizement."[8]

We might suggest, then, that it is hope's disposition to appreciate the present without absolutizing it which explains hope's middle course between inactivity and the excesses of overaction. Fromm's ideas show a remarkable similarity to those of Lynch and Marcel, as is seen, for example, in Fromm's development of the view that hope is neither passive waiting nor the unrealistic forcing of circumstances that cannot occur:

> To hope means to be ready at every moment for that which is not yet born, and yet not become desperate if there is no birth in our lifetime. There is no sense in hoping for that which already exists or for that which cannot be. Those whose hope is weak settle down for comfort or for violence; those whose hope is strong see and cherish all signs of new life and are ready every moment to help the birth of that which is ready to be born.[9]

Where there is no hope or where hopes have been shattered, people readjust their expectations and "reduce their demands to what they can get and do not even dream of that which seems to be out of their reach." After a while those without hope begin to lose their love of life, and because we cannot live without hope those who have lost hope often come to hate life and thus seek to destroy it in a spirit of violence. The real evil of hopelessness lies right here in the inability to live life, to act, and to plan for life.[10]

It is no exaggeration to say that hope changes a person's whole perspective on reality. This point has been well illustrated by Paul Pruyser who has written extensively in the field of religious psychology. Pruyser argues that for those who object to hope, reality is defined in terms of the past and the present, while for the person of hope, reality takes on the quality of "experience-in-formation." The objector to hope says, in effect, "You may as well abandon hope for things have never turned out that way." Without hope, reality means "things as they are" and "things past," along with their logical extrapolations, whereas the hopeful person assumes a different attitude toward time, and thus toward reality. With hope, one lives life as an adventure and sees reality as pregnant with resources yet undiscovered and untapped. With the time perspective shifted to the future, time as well as reality, is seen as an "ongoing process, very much on the move, with the possibility that novelty may occur, precisely because all reality has not yet been exhaustively defined."[11]

Hope surely involves a gifted vision, but it is most important that hope not be interpreted as an accompaniment or result of any kind of gnostic initiation. Marcel's position on this point is quite clear:

> . . . "I hope" cannot ever be taken to imply: "I am in the secret, I know the purpose of God or of the gods, whilst you are a profane outsider; and moreover it is because I have the benefit of special enlightenment that I say what I do." Such an interpretation is as unfair and inaccurate as it is possible to be, it does not take into account all that there is of humility, of timidity, of **chastity** in the true character of hope.[12]

Thus, hope is forced to hold a steady course between Scylla and Charybdis. It must resist every temptation to surround itself with the haughty cloak of gnosticism, and yet it must remain firm in its resolve not to allow its expectations to be dictated by rationalistic investigations.

28

To hope is, as we have seen, to have within oneself an assurance that the present intolerable situation cannot be final; there must be a way out. This assurance, moreover, is not simply an overlay upon personal inertia. Rather, as Marcel observes, "the being who hopes is putting forth a sort of interior activity."[13] This interior activity enables people to establish a proper relationship between self and the rest of reality which far exceeds their reach. It is this relational quality which explains the elements of modesty, humility, and even chastity, in hope and gives expression to hope's communal nature, the effect of which is to aid us in resisting the narcissistic exaggerations of human existence. Hope is a reality that is found and shared; it is given and received. "One hopes with, through and sometimes for someone else."[14]

Now, if hope is modest and humble, and if it bears what Marcel refers to as the mark of "inviolable timidity," we must necessarily wonder what it is that moves hope finally into action. Marcel is quick to suggest that the only way for the patience of hope to guard against its own degradation, its fall into weakness and complacency, is for it to remain ever faithful to "the principle of charity which should animate it."[15] The betrayal of love leads to the demise of hope, for hope is not held for oneself alone. Hope's presence within us is a flame which produces a radiance around us and only in this way is it kept alive within our own being.[16]

Quite simply, it seems, a person's modest regard of self in the light of hope liberates human energies for the development and nurturing of loving relationships that were once considered impossible.[17] While we shall have more to say later of the relationship between hope and Christian ethical reflection, we must suggest here that insofar as hope is communal and fosters an awareness of, and concern for, others, its place in Christian ethics is needed, even if not yet sufficiently assured. Moreover, within the context of Christianity, we have to insist that the communal understanding of hope is more than accidental or provisional, because the Christian's hope is rooted in a community of faith whose authenticity demands, and is tested by, that community's unending efforts to expand the compass of its care through the strains of love.

Up to now we have painted the picture of hope with broad strokes in an effort to disclose the elements which shape it. Hope does not lie in passive waiting, nor does it spend itself in a passion for activity. Hope is a personal inner action, something we do, but it is also an activity to which we are called; it is something we do in communion with our fellow humans. Finally, hope is patient and modest; it is moved to action only by the love which is its motivation. It is time now to draw in some of the finer lines of hope in order to catch a glimpse of its inner fabric, and to discover some of the effects that hope can have in shaping the life of society. In this way, we will also further lay bare the foundations of Christian hope and the questions it entails.

Fundamental Hope and the Question of Transcendence

An excellent phenomenological-philosophical description of lived hope has been given by Josef Pieper, who suggests that hope may at root be described as a joyous expectation of some good which is seen as possible of attainment, but not as inevitable. Indeed, since there is no need to hope for what we know will inevitably happen, we must suggest that we properly speak of hope only in relation to something that is not easily obtained, something that does not "already lie within reach of the outstretched hand; something that might still be denied to us, although we do not really doubt that we will obtain it."[18] To the extent that the object of hope is a "**bonum arduum**," an undeniable element of hope is the realization that ultimately the object of our hope is not at our disposal, not within our power alone, no matter how enduring our efforts to bring that object under our control. To say otherwise is to betray the experience of hope, at least in its most authentic form.[19]

This last qualification indicates that there is some variation to the spectrum of human experiences which pass as expressions of the reality of hope. This is indeed the case. Nor is the situation with hope unique. The same plurality of experiences is seen in the phenomenon of love. While we recognize a variety of forms of love, a reference to "lovers" usually signifies a particular kind of love, an erotic love. So too, there is a special significance to the designation, "person of hope." As Pieper explains it, "there are a thousand hopes that man can abandon and lose without thereby becoming absolutely 'hopeless'; but there is a single hope, the hope for one thing, whose loss would signify that a person no longer had any hope whatsoever and was absolutely 'without hope'."[20]

Marcel gives recognition to the different forms of hope in the distinction he makes between the statement "I hope that . . . . ," and the absolute or unconditioned statement, "I hope . . . ."[21] In the latter statement no attempt is made to predict the state of affairs that will prevail. Instead, one simply confesses to being a person of fundamental hope. It is at the moment of disappointment of our many hopes that this fundamental hope most often appears. In the experience of disappointment the way is opened for the purging of all illusory hopes. Thus disappointment is really a liberation from an illusion, an illusion which consists, as Pieper says, "in our imagining that the acquisition of certain goods in the world of objects, including physical health, constitutes salvation for our existence, or is at least a necessary component of it." Strangely enough, then, in disillusionment and disappointment of our many hopes we become consciously aware, perhaps for the first time, of what we have secretly known all along—that we have hoped with all our being for "something else." And so, in this way, disappointment is a summons "to enter into this ampler area of existence: the area of hope **per se**."[22]

Insofar as fundamental hope involves a quest for something whose attainment is never entirely within our power, Pieper is critical of any attempt to translate the concept of hope into a political program where efforts are undertaken and plans made for the realization of one's hope in this world. Thus he obviously disagrees with the belief that all meaningful hopes can and must be realized by an exclusive dependence upon the socialistic transformation begun in the Marxist revolution.[23] But at this point we have to balance Pieper's opposition to human or political planning with the suggestion that while we are finally unable to attain our hope's fulfillment on our own, we can never abandon the task of cultivating an atmosphere conducive for the realization of this hope.

This brings us to focus on a basic point of difference between the Christian and the Marxist views of hope and the role of human beings in the struggle to see their hopes fulfilled. In contrast to the Marxist vision of an idealized "heaven on earth" that is gradually achieved in the evolutionary development of history, Pieper subscribes to Marcel's belief that human hope is directed finally toward salvation and that "salvation is nothing if it does not free us from death."[24] For Pieper, this means that no future state of being can seriously claim to be an object of human hope if it ignores the reality of death in which each of us must come to have a part.

31

Whether we speak in Marxist terms of a classless society or in Teilhard's terms of a new level of cosmic consciousness and human unanimity, Pieper insists that real hope must free us from death, that is, it must affect our personal fate on the other side of death, for whatever else human existence is, it is also an existence unto death.[25]

This is not to say, however, that the expectation of hope's fulfillment on the other side of death can be facilely written off as "other-worldliness," because it is precisely this world, this creation, which the Christian person of hope expects will "pass through death and disaster in order to achieve perfection." Moreover, quite basically, the Christian is convinced, as Pieper puts it, "that the frontier of death between the here and the beyond has in a certain sense already been breached, from that other shore, through that event hidden behind the theological term 'Incarnation'."[26] And an even greater breakthrough has been achieved, we might add, through the mysterious event of Christ's Resurrection.

Yet even for the Christian, human history establishes the boundaries for the expression of the social aspects of hope, and death presents itself as the frontier for hope in its personal dimensions. Whether we like it or not, death stands as an absolute and final limit to our worldly hopes. Thus Juan Alfaro can say that any lasting success in burying death beneath a growing pile of worldly hopes is simply out of the question, for death, by being present in anticipation, makes our whole existence, our decisions, and our actions in the world, relative. [27] It is at the moment of death that we confront at last our total inability to save ourselves through our own resources, and once and for all the fatal illusion of our human self-sufficiency is put to rest.

By its very appearance as a brush with nothingness, death thus becomes a frontier, a boundary, of the transcendent, a call to our inner depths to take the decision of hope. Realizing now our inability to render our own existence secure, we can only hope for the gift of a new existence. And so, as Alfaro sees it, in the presence of death we are faced with the option "between an autonomous existence limited to its possibilities in this world . . . , and a brave open existence trusting in hope of a transcendent future. Death, then, is a frontier for man's freedom in the option it places before him between hoping and not hoping beyond the scope of this world." The issue is clear-drawn: there is simply no way for us to make the crossing to an extra-mundane existence on our own; nor does the evidence of our own reasoning provide a guarantee to the presence of life after death. But one thing must be emphasized and insisted upon: the call to hope really does not issue from the mouth of death only at the moment of our entering into it. Rather, "because death is permanently present in human existence, the whole of life is a frontier of hope."[28] Thus, it is the whole of human existence that reveals itself as a call to hope so that long before the final option at the moment of death we are prepared and conditioned to make the last of our decisions.

It so happens that from the depths of our human consciousness hope emerges as a call, a summons, "to take the radical and totalizing decision of existence." In the end we either define the meaning of our life in terms of a fulfillment received, accepted and appreciated as a gift, or we face the prospect of spending ourselves in the process of an autonomous self-realization without fulfillment. We live either with hopes limited to this world, or we hope fully; in the latter event we catch sight of a future which we cannot create on our own, but which can only come to us as grace.[29] The effects in our lives of this fundamental, or what Avery Dulles refers to as transcendent, hope are nothing short of liberating and inspiring. Listen to Dulles:

> Transcendent hope, by placing man's true security beyond anything this world can give or take away, bestows a sovereign freedom of action . . . . It helps to cure the weakness which undermines our best efforts . . . . A transcendent hope, freeing us from pessimism and anxiety, would enable us to commit ourselves generously and enthusiastically to the task before us and, if necessary, to accept what, in the eyes of men, appears to be defeat.[30]

As we conclude this section of our investigation into hope, we remind ourselves that there are two major kinds of hope; one has to do with ordinary hopes of everyday, while the other enfolds itself around the very heart of human existence. Or we may speak, as Jan Peters does, of a relatively short-term hope, and of one which is long-term. The first is warranted by a degree of rational insight and understanding. Because this short-term kind of hope enjoys a degree of probability or calculated chance and involves only a reduced risk, it "calls for less moral courage, less of the resolve needed for taking the plunge into the gap presented by the future." By way of contrast, however, fundamental or transcendent "hope in the longer term presupposes an unshakable faith, an awareness of the risks and a readiness to allow, on an existential basis, for the possibility that outwardly the vision may be lost. Yet it sharpens that faculty of vision which tradition knows as 'the eye of faith'."[31]

Insofar as even "the eye of faith" is powerless to deny the reality of the present situation's pain, it is imperative that the future envisaged in hope should always involve an ending to the alienation of the present, whether that future be some sort of Promethean self-made utopia or the kingdom of God so desired by Christians. But whereas the utopian has no expectations apart from the successful employment of his own resourcefulness as directed against present evils, in Christian hope we labor, **full of expectancy**, for a new creation which will liberate us from existing servitudes. Invariably, as Christians we are enabled, and seem drawn, to respond to things beyond our seeing, things beyond our hearing, things beyond our imagining—all prepared by God for those who love him (I Cor. 2:9). In the final analysis, then, Christian hope, as Louis Dupré would have it, "is not based upon moral wisdom or confidence in human power but upon an eschatological intervention of the transcendent."[32] Because of this fact, and because such an intervention is unrecognizable except in the light of faith, we must now explore in some detail the meaning of faith and the role it plays in its relationship to hope.

Faith, Knowledge and Hope

In this section of our study we intend to illustrate the theological significance of hope as it has taken shape within Christianity. To do this, we must necessarily relate hope to the faith in which it is grounded and without which it is senseless and naive. At its root, the theology of hope represents the recovery of a basic theme in the Judeo-Christian tradition which views faith as the acceptance of God and his promise, and thus from the very start contains within itself an element of hope for the fulfillment of that promise. Indeed, as Dulles remarks, in the New Testament it is practically synonymous to be a believer and to be a person of hope, so that St. Paul can describe the Gentiles as those "other people who have no hope" (1 Thess. 4:13).[33] Moreover, Paul's teaching that we are justified by faith (Rom. 3:28) does not prevent him from adding that as of now we are saved, "though only in hope" (Rom. 3:24). Faith, indeed, "gives substance to our hopes, and makes us certain of realities we do not see" (Heb. 11:1). Thus, it is neither strange, nor without warrant, that today some theologians choose to portray Christian theology not exclusively as "faith seeking understanding," but also as "hope seeking understanding."

Juan Alfaro depicts Christian hope as an exercise of "existence in exodus" by which we go out of ourselves and renounce any guarantee of salvation afforded by human calculation.[34] Rather, our trust lies in God and in his promise to be Emmanuel whereby he may assist us in our labors at fidelity to the work entrusted to us. In fact, it is not unfair to suggest, as Dulles does, that "in a certain sense, man has a hope because he has a mission. Because God has committed a task to man, man can be sure that God will be with those who faithfully perform their mission and that he will crown their efforts in the end."[35] The moorings of all assurance in our own self-sufficiency and in that of the world are broken, and as Christians we toss the anchor of our hope "into the bottomless depths of the mystery of God in Christ." Thus in speaking of the Christian, Alfaro says:

> In the act of hoping he lives the experience of being loved by God; he is conscious (with an a-thematic knowledge) of God's love for him. This is the certainty of Christian hope: certainty that God is for me the God of grace, a certainty lived (not reflected) in the very decision to hope; a certainty which grasps the promise and thus tends towards the salvation to come. "Justification by faith" means "salvation in hope" (Rom. 5:1-5; 8:24-25).[36]

This is sufficient indication, I think, of the fundamental relationship which faith bears to Christian hope. The mere acknowledgment of this relationship, however, is inadequate to our needs and purposes, for we have suggested that hope is the dynamism of human and Christian existence, a dynamism which explains the persistence of our historical struggle for fulfillment and transcendence, whether this fulfillment be interpreted finally in terms of natural law teleology or in eschatological terms. To say simply that hope is rooted in faith may explain the existence of hope, but it says precious little of the vitality of hope. Something is still missing, and we must try to approach the heart of the matter.

Marcuse once observed that "men can die without anxiety if they know that what they love is protected from misery and oblivion."[37] The same sentiment was earlier expressed by Teilhard de Chardin when he remarked to the effect that we cannot live and work unless we know that the fruits of our life and labor shall perdure.[38] What is noteworthy in both these statements is the reference to our need for some kind of knowledge of the future. Indeed, such knowledge must be seen as the condition for our ability both to face the future with confidence and hope and to labor for its coming. In short, the dynamism of hope involves a knowledge of the future which in some way affords us a grasp upon that future. Our task now is to explore the nature of such knowledge, how it is possible, and how it is mediated in the dynamism of Christian hopefulness. It is our contention that knowledge of the future comes into focus within the relationship which is Christian faith, and that this faith is indeed the medium, the meeting-ground, for knowledge and hope.

Daniel Day Williams has discussed the dynamic tension existing between knowing and hoping as these realities take root in the phenomenon of Christian faith. The Christian lives in light of a promise of future fulfillment—"You shall know the truth and the truth will make you free"—but this promise is meaningless apart from the belief in, and acceptance of, the faithfulness of God and of his personal Word, Jesus Christ, who is already the way, the life, and the truth. What we hope for, then, is closely bound up with our knowledge of who God is and of what our life comes to mean in view of God's concern for us. Thus, Williams argues that while we live as Christians "in a dimension of expectation which stretches into the future and beyond death . . . . we hope on the basis of a knowledge of our real situation before and with God." We are now children of God, but it does not yet appear what we shall be. We are already a new creation in Christ Jesus, but we do not yet know how this creation will be colored and shaped in its final glory except that "we shall be like him."[39]

Clearly, reality grounds the Christian's hope, but this reality is a relational one which takes shape within the experience of faith, and it is only within the context of this experience that Christianity and Christian ethics are formed. Thus, when we turn to the question of whether or not it is reasonable for us to be hopeful in the conduct of our lives, we do not find it strange that in the experiences both of personal human trust and of the theological virtue of hope, "the relationship comes first and the evidence comes second, produced or illuminated by the relationship." Or, more accurately, we might say that the relationship transforms the evidence, so that what formerly pointed only to the despair of ambivalence, now "proves the possibility of hope and freedom . . ."[40] The point to be stressed here is that the decision both for human trust and for religious hope can never depend totally on the evidence of what is seen, for if we insist on waiting until all the evidence is in before we commit ourselves to trusting and hoping, we will simply never make the commitment. Like it or not, it is the actual experience of trusting and hoping which gives the evidence its structural existence and weight, and this is really only a nonbiblical way of saying that "hope that is seen is not hope, for who hopes for that which he sees" (Rom. 8:24).

The willingness to accept the fact that trust and hope transform the evidence for their own justification depends upon a prior disposition to accept the possibility that what really moves us to trust and to hope, just as to faith, is not so much **what** is evidenced, but **who** provides the evidence, not **what** is said, but **who** says it. We are moved, in other words, by the testimony of the witness, and this means, finally, by the person of the witness. In some way, for some reason, we are won over by the person bearing witness, and we are moved to respond in openness, trust, and hope, but always with some sense of abandonment, of "letting go" of self, in that all the reasons for our response defy demonstration or precise verification. This is the situation both in our trust in our neighbor, and in our faith and hope in God. Still, for the person who has come to believe, to trust, and to hope, just as for the person who has come to love, the gateway to new dimensions of experience is opened, and reality's horizons are more richly colored and expansive.

Being more than just an intellectual assent, faith is rather a total personal response to, and acceptance of, another person. As such it involves openness, trust, gratitude and obedience. Just as in our other personal relationships, so also in our relationship with God, we cannot know him in a truly personal way unless he freely manifests himself to us in our openness to him, for personal knowledge demands and presupposes some kind of immediate and direct relationship. It is only the graciousness of God in turning toward us in a personal way that changes the order of things and makes possible our faithful response as whole, human and reasonable beings.

As a fully human response to God, faith is surely reasonable, but the element of decision is unavoidable; faith remains an option. By freeing ourselves to have faith in another human being, we are well prepared for religious faith as the personal response made in freedom to the person of Christ as the witness of God. In both human and religious faith the will of the believer is directed toward the person of the witness, but insofar as this witness testifies to a reality which is not fully accessible to the natural processes of human thought, he will be convincing only to the extent that we have made up our minds that we want to believe him. In other words, in the long tradition of Augustine, Thomas, Kierkegaard, Newman and Marcel, we must be willing to believe. Thus, integral to faith is an openness to the reality of personal encounter.[41] Put simply, this means that for Christians, the vitality of religious faith depends upon the reality of the personal and communal presence of Christ in the here-and-now. It is because we find it possible to respond to the person of Christ as he is today, that we also can have faith in the promises he fleshed out in the past, and can live in hopeful anticipation of their fulfillment in the future.

Thus it is within the faith-experience, or what must more accurately and more revealingly be termed the faith-relationship, that Christian hope comes to life. If our hope is not arbitrary and naive, we must insist that neither may our faith be such. In other words, faith itself is rooted in an experience which affords us a kind of knowledge by means of which we come to be assured that our hope is not in vain. This knowledge, in light of the kind of faith which we have just described, can best be called a personal knowledge or, better still, an interpersonal knowledge. To recognize faith as the grace or gift which it is, means simply that we must await the free self-giving or spontaneous self-manifestation of God in Christ to us. Rooted in personal knowledge or knowledge of a person, faith offers a kind of certainty which has neither benefit nor need of demonstration. Its conviction and assurance are built more upon the basis of shared love and mutual insight than upon proven premises and logical deductions. Such knowledge as this can be shaken finally only by the experience of personal infidelity.

Hope As A Communal Reality

Having explored the role which faith plays in the birth of hope, we are now in a position to understand more fully the essentially communitarian character of hope. One question of life to which hope is an answer is whether or not solitude is the last word. Hope's response is a resounding no. The case for hope arises in faith, and in the intersubjectivity and love which faith implies. In this regard, Marcel speaks of hope as an experience in which we open ourselves to a communion which leads both to our own regeneration and to that of our neighbors.[42] How integral faith is to hope's experience of communion is seen in Marcel's judgment that "hope cannot be separated either from a sense of communion or from a more or less conscious and explicit dependence on a power which guarantees this communion itself. 'I hope in Thee, for us', such is the authentic formula of hope."[43] The "Thou" in whom the believer hopes is "in some way the guarantee of the union which holds us together, myself to myself, or the one to the other, or these beings to those other beings."[44]

In and through belief in the person of the "Thou," people of hope decide that reality intends the fulfillment and not the frustration of the human spirit. There lies within hope an implicit belief in the existence of a beneficent force which uses its power to establish the shape of reality, and in fact to create novelty. This beneficent force transcends the knowledge which is distilled from the past and present, and in this way it establishes itself as the power of the future.[45] In light of this beneficence, people of hope dare to abandon any attitude of defensive reactionism, and to relate to reality in a spirit of responsive creativity and loving initiative. For Christians, of course, the beneficence of reality reveals itself in the person of a provident God who makes his intention clear in the form of the eschatological promises and in their fulfillment for Jesus Christ in the mysterious events of his life, death, and resurrection.

With their vision of hope, Christians find themselves carried "beyond death" in the sense that reality is seen as having a larger compass than was previously suspected. Although they live toward the future, they do so without ignoring the present and the past. In fact, because hoping is concerned with the realization of possibilities and promises, and not simply with theoretical potentialities, nothing so assists anyone in sustaining hope as the fulfillment of past promises and present hopes. In other words, the climate most conducive to hope is one which is ripe with tension between what has already been actualized and what still remains as only possible.[46]

Faith is always the basis of Christian hope, but hope is the life of faith; it is the mood which faith inspires. With the vision of faith, hope understands the present as a time of pregnancy, and from this knowledge hope draws the courage, not to die, but to live, and to maintain the struggle against the vanities of empty optimism and the threats of sterile pessimism. As people of hope, of course, we expect neither heaven on earth nor any other kind of utopia within history, but what we do expect and intend to achieve is a usable future.[47] We do not hesitate to look at the depths and dregs of human reality, while at the same time hoping against hope, knowing, as it were, "that the final victory belongs to God as the power of the future and to Christ as the one who has removed 'the deadliness of death'."[48]

Concluding Remarks: Hope and Help

Once again the time has come to draw together the threads of our discussion. We have spoken in this chapter of human hope and of the work of imagination which makes it possible for us to see reality in its proper perspective and thus to evaluate it in a realistic way. As the ally and agent of hope, the human imagination resists our tendency to absolutize the present situation. Imagination succeeds in its work by means of a twofold process: first, it fights its way through fantasy and fiction into the facts of reality, and then it affords a perspective which establishes these facts in a context, guaranteeing, thereby, that they do not remain as scattered absolutes which would only preoccupy and frighten us.[49]

We have made much of faith's role in the experience of hope, for from its origin in faith we obtain an insight into hope's inner structure. Hope is an interior possession, but it is not exclusively such, especially insofar as this interiority might be taken to imply total self-possession and autonomy. Rather, we approach the heart of hope when we appreciate that it, like faith, is a relational reality. In an elementary way, hope may be described as the fundamental knowledge and feeling that there is a way out of present difficulties. But in the Christian dispensation it must be added immediately that to discover and to effect this way out, invariably requires assistance.

40

Thus, while hope is undoubtedly an interior strength, since it is not at the same time also self-sufficient and omnipotent, it must, as Lynch says, "rediscover the other half of itself, the outside world and the idea of help."[50] To the extent that we find it difficult to accept the fact that help is basic to the idea of humanity, we will probably resist the definition of hope in terms of help. Nevertheless, we must insist that while hope is truly on the inside of us, it is really "an interior sense that there is help on the outside of us."[51] In the trying experiences of life, as people of hope we are aware of our real human limitations, but we also anticipate the possibilities of rescue, and thus we search the horizons whence help may come.

So long as we persist in contriving to repress the need for help and to deny that help is part of the nature of hope, we succeed only in disposing ourselves to become victims of hopelessness, not necessarily in its grossest forms of catatonic despair and inactivity, but in its disguised shapes of overactivity, boastfulness, arrogance, and even violence. Lynch believes that if human energy is to be conserved and channeled into its more creative outlets, we must develop a realistic sense of the possible, and this entails of necessity an accurate awareness of what is impossible.[52] On both the individual and communal levels, we can and must distinguish between what is humanly hopeless and what is hopeful, which is really another way of saying that we can and must recognize and acknowledge that there are situations, personal and social, which cry for healing assistance.

This, it seems, is both a psychological, as well as a theological, truth. If we successfully single out the areas of personal and social hopelessness, and thus prevent them from dulling or distorting the sharpness of the areas of possibility, we will show more initiative and creative response in the task of helping both others and ourselves. Lynch has noted that an accurate sense of the possible is a psychological boon in that "to keep the two, the possible and the impossible, in place is to stay free of intolerable burdens."[53] This sense of the possible, however, is also a theological and an ethical necessity. It arises within the experience of hope and explains the hopeful Christian's ability to walk the line between expectant waiting and the passion for activity; it preserves the individual's integrity and initiative, but always within the context of social responsibility; and finally it frees the patience and modesty of hope to answer the demands of love which call out for hope to prove itself, now in action, now in restraint.

41

Within the context of Christianity what, then, can be said of hope? It is, first of all, invincible in that it rests in God who is both loving and powerful, and thus can offer us good things and make good on his promises. Secondly, there is no temptation for Christians to pretend that suffering and death are illusions. We are realistic enough to appreciate that participation in these painful events is the prelude to sharing in an awaited glory. But this glorious future is not the reward or outcome simply of endless worldly progress. Thirdly, Christian hope is fruitful. There is no alienated fascination with the eternal such that the things of time lose their interest and importance. Personal, social and cosmic redemption call for human involvement. As Christians we do not condemn this world, but neither do we expect through our own planning and resourcefulness the successful building of God's kingdom here on earth. Still, we must labor and suffer, like our Lord, in selfless love. And yet, because our hope is transcendent, we know that it is not necessary for our efforts to be attended always by what passes in the world for success. Nor are we shocked by the possibility or reality of worldly rejection and humiliation.[54]

Just as with faith and with love, so also, then, at the root of hope there is something which is literally offered to us; but we can refuse hope no less than we can refuse faith and love. For such a refusal, however, we pay the high price, both of our humanity and of our efforts at Christianity. Without hope, moreover, the ethical reflections of Christians are deprived of a dynamism whose formal influence upon theological ethics will concern us throughout the remainder of this study.

CHAPTER II

REFERENCES

1. Erich Fromm, The Revolution of Hope. Toward A Humanized Technology (New York: Bantam Books, 1968), p. 2.

2. Ibid., p. 98.

3. Ibid., pp. 3-4.

4. Ibid., pp. 6-8.

5. Ibid., p. 8.

6. William F. Lynch, S.J., Images of Hope: Imagination as Healer of the Hopeless (New York: Mentor-Omega Books, 1966), pp. 27-9. Lynch relies here upon the work of Kurt Levin, Field Theory in Social Science, Selected Papers, ed. Dorwin Cartwright (New York: Harper Torchbooks, 1951), p. 53.

7. Gabriel Marcel, Homo Viator: Introduction to a Metaphysics of Hope, trans. Emma Craufurd (New York: Harper Torchbooks, 1962), p. 52.

8. Leslie Farber, M.D., in his introduction to Lynch, Images, p. viii.

9. Fromm, Revolution, p. 9.

10. Ibid., pp. 21-5.

11. Paul W. Pruyser, A Dynamic Psychology of Religion. (New York: Harper & Row, 1968), p. 168; also his article, "Phenomenology and Dynamics of Hoping," Journal for the Scientific Study of Religion, III (Fall, 1963), 86-96 at 91.

12. Marcel, Homo Viator, p. 35.

13. Gabriel Marcel, The Mystery of Being, vol. 2: Faith and Reality, trans. René Hague (Chicago: Henry Regnery Co., 1960), pp. 178-79.

14. Pruyser, "Phenomenology," p. 95.

15. Marcel, Homo Viator, pp. 50-1, 40.

16. Marcel, The Mystery of Being, vol. 2, p. 179.

17. Pruyser, "Phenomenology," p. 95.

18. Josef Pieper, Hope and History, trans. Richard and Clara Winston (New York: Herder & Herder, 1969), pp. 19-21. Pieper refers to the discussion of "hope" in Johannes Hoffmeister, Wörterbuch der philosophischen Begriffe (Hamburg, 2nd ed., 1955), p.304.

19. Ibid., pp. 21-2 where Pieper quotes Marcel: "The only genuine hope is that which is directed toward something not dependent on ourselves." See Marcel, Position et approches concrètes du mystère ontologique (Paris, 1949), p. 73.

20. Ibid., p. 23. This difference appears in French in the distinction between espoir, which occurs most often in plural forms, and espérance, which practically excludes the plural form.

21. Marcel, Homo Viator, p. 32.

22. Pieper, Hope, pp. 26-7.

23. Ibid., p. 68.

24. Marcel, The Mystery of Being, vol. 2, p. 202; referred to by Pieper, Hope, p. 70.

25. Pieper, Hope, pp. 73-4.

26. Ibid., pp. 87-8.

27. Juan Alfaro, "Christian Hope and the Hopes of Mankind," Dimensions of Spirituality, Concilium Series, Vol. 59, ed. Christian Duquoc (New York: Herder & Herder, 1970), pp. 59-69 at 61-3.

28. Ibid., pp. 62-63.

29. Ibid., pp. 59-61.

30. Avery Dulles, S.J., "An Apologetics of Hope," The God Experience. Essays in Hope, ed. Joseph P. Whelan, S.J. (New York: Newman Press: 1971), pp. 244-63 at 252-53.

31. Jan Peters, "Black Theology as a Sign of Hope," Dimensions of Spirituality, pp. 112-24 at 113.

32. Louis Dupré, "Hope and Transcendence," The God Experience, pp. 217-25 at 219-20.

33. Dulles, "Apologetics of Hope," p. 246.

34. Alfaro, "Christian Hope," p. 67.

35. Dulles, "Apologetics of Hope," pp. 258-59.

36. Alfaro, "Christian Hope," p. 67.

37. Herbert Marcuse, Eros and Civilization (Boston: Beacon Press, 1955), p. 236.

38. Pierre Teilhard de Chardin, The Vision of the Past, trans. J.M. Cohen (New York: Harper & Row, 1966), pp. 232-33.

39. Daniel Day Williams, "Knowing and Hoping in the Christian Faith," The God Experience, pp. 168-89 at 170-71.

40. Lynch, Images of Hope, p. 106.

41. Ingo Hermann, The Experience of Faith, trans. Daniel Coogan (New York: Kenedy and Sons, 1966), Chap. 3.

42. Marcel, Homo Viator, p. 67.

43. Ibid., p. 93.

44. Ibid., pp. 60-1.

45. Pruyser, Dynamic Psychology, p. 168. The basic benevolence of reality is also acknowledged by H. Richard Niebuhr, The

Responsible Self. An Essay in Christian Moral Philosophy (New York: Harper & Row, 1963), pp. 175-78 and *passim*.

46. Pruyser, "Phenomenology," p. 91.

47. Martin E. Marty, *The Search for a Usable Future* (New York: Harper & Row, 1969), p. 61; also Ch. 2, pp. 26-40.

48. *Ibid.*, p. 65.

49. Lynch, *Images*, p. 209.

50. *Ibid.*, p. 24.

51. *Ibid.*, p. 31.

52. *Ibid.*, p. 47.

53. *Ibid.*, p. 51.

54. Dulles, "Apologetics of Hope," pp. 253-57.

CHAPTER III
REDEEMED TO LOVE THROUGH HOPE:
TEILHARD'S DYNAMIC MORALITY OF CONQUEST

Introduction

Our first concern in this chapter will be to uncover the shaping forces of Teilhard's theology; it will become clear that by seeking a reconciliation between the Christian's faith in God and his faith in human endeavor, Teilhard offers a response to humanism's critical view of religion, and at the same time prepares a theological basis for viewing Christian action as a participation in the creative and redemptive work of Christ. After developing Teilhard's arguments for the basic unity of the major mysteries of Christianity, an extensive analysis will be provided of his views on evil and sin, especially in their cosmic foundations. An understanding of Teilhard's views on original sin and the individual's personal appropriation of the forces of evil is crucial for an appreciation of the theory he proposes of Christ's redemption as primarily a positive action of creative unification and only secondarily an act of reparation or expiation for sin. In this perspective, our redemption comes to be seen as a movement out of hopelessness into hope; morality, moreover, takes shape, for Teilhard, as an energetic conquest by means of which we labor to construct the earth according to the requirements of Christian love that serves as the law both of the individual's personalization and of human socialization. But the foundation of this love, the source of its energy, and the secret of its persistence, is the reality of Christian hope which serves as its dynamism.

The Legacy and Fundamental Mold of Teilhard's Theology

Teilhard de Chardin lived with the basic conviction that his "faith in God" and his "faith in the world" were ultimately at one in Jesus Christ. Many of his writings in fact are successive efforts to express and clarify, on one level or another, this overriding insight: that the conflict between the Christian mysticism of "the Upward" and the humanist mysticism of "the Forward" is only apparent. Thus, without unfairness to the general thrust of his thinking and writing, Teilhard's legacy and unique contribution to contemporary

Christianity may be judged to lie in his synthesis of a vertically moving faith in God and a horizontally moving faith in the world and its future.[1]

Teilhard entitled one of his essays "The Heart of the Problem" to indicate that the basic cause of Christianity's troubles is its failure to come to grips with the tension rooted more or less consciously in the human spirit as a result of the apparent conflict between the modern **forward impulse** of technological progress and the more traditional **upward impulse** of religious worship. The question must be answered: Are we to turn above or ahead, or in both directions? The solution is clear for Teilhard: the choice is not a simple alternative, for the upward and forward forces are weakened and wither away in separation from each other. The forces, rather, must be combined so that humanity may move upward by moving forward, and forward by moving upward. The combination of these forces is essential not only to humanity's well-being, but would also help to remedy the ineffectualness of Christianity's missionary activity which is due, claims Teilhard, to the fact that Christian charity lacks "the sensitizing ingredient of **Human** faith and hope," as a result of which Christianity must appear as "colorless, cold and inassimilable."[2]

Teilhard attributes the tension which marks the action and thinking of the modern age to two currents of psychic energy that he speaks of as two forms of faith. On one hand, there are spiritualists (particularly Christians) for whom faith in God is a distraction from any hope or yearning to achieve some kind of "super-humanity;" on the other hand, there are materialists (particularly Marxists) for whom any appeal to God or "transcendent finality" is interpreted as a compromise and an affront to their faith in humanity. Teilhard calls for a mutual openness between these two forms of faith, not that either should be compromised, but that their synthesis might produce a single resultant energy. His own evolutionary system is presented, in fact, as the focus of reconciliation for the upward and forward forces of faith.

There is, according to Teilhard, a simultaneity between the end or goal of history and the beginning of eternity. In a momentary paroxysm of energy, humanity and the universe reach final maturation, and at that instant the Parousia of Christ unfolds. This moment of human maturation is a necessary but, in itself, insufficient condition for the arrival of the Parousia, which can never be understood simply as the product or result of human endeavor.[3] In light of this coincidence between the points of planetary maturation (the forward movement) and the Parousia (the upward movement), Teilhard concludes that there should be no radical opposition between the two movements of faith which they inspire: "Some (the old-fashioned Christians) say: Await the return of Christ. Others (the Marxists) reply: Achieve the World. And the third (the neo-Catholics) think: In order that Christ can return we must **achieve** the World."[4]

Teilhard is here trying to infuse the traditional Christian doctrine of eschatology with those elements of human faith and hope so sorely needed today. In keeping with this intention he further suggests that we stop viewing the Parousia, the consummation of God's kingdom, as a purely catastrophic event, one, that is, which is liable to occur at any moment regardless of the state of humanity at that time. Instead, in keeping with his theory of anthropogenesis, and "in perfect analogy with the mystery of the first Christmas which . . . could only have happened between Heaven and an Earth which was **prepared**, socially, politically and psychologically, to receive Jesus," Teilhard proposes the hypothesis "that the parousiac spark can, of physical and organic necessity, only be kindled between Heaven and a mankind which has biologically reached a certain critical evolutionary point of collective maturity."[5]

This means, in effect, that we can move toward the zenith of Christian faith and the crowning of the Incarnation only by moving toward the horizon of human faith, the natural completion of humanity's evolutionary growth. Teilhard is committed to the possibility of believing "**at the same time and wholly** in God **and** the World, the one through the other," because Christ is the Redeemer, not only in the sense of being the Savior of individuals, but also as the Mover of anthropogenesis. And so, the resultant movement of humanity—upward by way of forward and forward by way of upward—, far from being a half-hearted compromise between heaven and earth, demands of us, on the contrary, two forms of detachment, two forms, that is, of "sacrifice to that which is greater than self."[6] We must spend ourselves for God and for the human community, for God through the community, and for the community through God.

Teilhard discovers the transcendent face of evolution in the person of Jesus Christ on whom the whole process depends, not only for its beginnings, but also for its continued development and for its

49

ultimate fulfillment. As the Person who is both the last term of the evolutionary series and who is also outside all series, Christ is both the auto-center and hypercenter of the process, and as such, he attracts human beings by love and brings them and their labors to fulfillment on the other side of the death barrier.[7] It is faith in the person of Jesus Christ as God and in his co-extensiveness with the whole of the creative evolutionary process that explains and, in a sense, completes Teilhard's faith in the world, and affords to his vision of the future outcome of evolution an element of hopeful certainty not possible on the basis of scientific extrapolations alone. The epistemological stability of his phenomenology rests ultimately on Christian revelation. He himself admits that he would never have envisaged what he calls the Omega Point as the summit of the evolutionary cone, nor postulated that hypothesis rationally, if his knowledge of Christ through Christian faith had not revealed to him, not only the Omega Point's speculative model, but also its living reality.[8]

The Unity of the Christian Mysteries

The development of Teilhard's speculative and practical synthesis of the Upward and the Forward involves three strands of thought, all of which must be kept in balance. On one level, Teilhard's thinking is a kind of scientific phenomenology which allows him to see the universe in the process of evolution according to the law of "complexity-consciousness": the level of consciousness is directly proportionate to the level of organization through unification which a being enjoys. Utilizing the energy of love, which Teilhard understands as internal or radial energy ("the within of things") and which, unlike external or tangential energy ("the without of things"), is not subject to the law of entropy, the movement of the universe is in the direction of greater spiritualization toward a point, a center, that is already in existence and is profoundly personal.

On a second level of thinking, Teilhard uses the data of Christian revelation and identifies this personal center toward which evolution is converging with Christ. In other words, "the personal center of convergent evolution, the new 'God of the Forward,' is the same as Christ, the incarnate traditional 'God of the Upward'."[9] At the third level, Teilhard outlines a positive morality, a Christian mystique of human conquest based directly on his Christology, not in the sense, however, that he develops a program of Christian ethics in any

systematic or comprehensive way. Nonetheless, Teilhard's writings are permeated by what can only be seen as a fundamental ethical concern. Indeed, that we discover a pervasive ethical dimension in his writings is not surprising, in that Teilhard sees the whole of Christianity as resting on, and being summed up by, a double dogma: "the physical primacy of Christ and the moral primacy of charity."[10]

Suffice it for now to say, that because Teilhard sees a certain co-existence and co-extension of Christ with the universe, he can speak of human effort as being a participation in God's continuous creative action and, more particularly, a participation in the redemptive action of Christ. The Christian and his or her activities are taken seriously. In a bold enterprise the Christian is called to work for the mutual completion of God and of the world. In other words, the redemptive value of human effort carried out in Christ is emphasized, and it is made clear that heaven is attained by building up the earth. In this sense, then, the Christian must be engaged in a dynamic morality of conquest, a movement toward union with God in and through the world, issuing finally in the total liberation of the individual and the whole human community.

Because of its organic unity it is often difficult to keep the various levels of Teilhard's thinking distinct. Nevertheless, in this chapter we are concerned mainly with the second and third levels, that is, with Teilhard's understanding of the meaning and role of Christ, and with his interpretation of the dynamism of a positive Christian morality. What is immediately evident in Teilhard's thinking is its cosmic scope. Christ is the foundation of the universe, and he is the source of intelligibility for all reality insofar as everything which was, is, and will be, is directed toward him, the goal and purpose of all creation. In addition to being both the basis and goal of the universe, Christ is the bond of union, the source of energy by means of which all things are to find their final fulfillment. With Christ as the basic fact—or better still, as the basic reality—, Teilhard has already shaken considerably the traditional habit of thinking in debilitating dichotomies. We may no longer facilely split the universe into matter and spirit; humans are not simply body and soul; things are not sacred and profane. The universe, rather, is personalized; everything in its own way shares in the person of Christ who is being fulfilled precisely in and by the efforts of all creatures to be themselves.[11]

Within the framework of this evolving personal universe two things may be said about the central mysteries of the Christian experience. First, Teilhard maintains that when the mysteries of creation, incarnation, and redemption are understood in their full sense they appear, not as facts which can be localized at a given point in time and space, but rather as "true dimensions of the world (not objects of perception, but a condition of all possible perceptions.)"[12] Secondly, these mysteries of Christianity are one with the continuing life-events of Jesus Christ, so that not only do they lose their meaning if isolated one from the others, but also they find their continuity and permanence only in the experience of Christ, an experience, moreover, which is still awaiting completion. For Teilhard, Christianity has awakened to the realization that its three fundamental mysteries are in fact simply three aspects of one and the same process, the building up of Christ (Christogenesis), "considered either in its motive principle (creation), or in its unifying mechanism (incarnation), or in its ascensional work (redemption)."[13]

The essential unity of the chief mysteries of Christianity is a theme which drew Teilhard's attention more than once in the course of his lifetime. Thus, for example, only a year after he wrote the above, he again returned to the subject to suggest that the three mysteries (creation, incarnation and redemption) of the establishment of Christ must be understood as related elements of that process which constitutes a fourth mystery of Christianity; it is the mystery of Pleromization or the creative unification of the world in God through Christ, the gradual unifying reduction of the original multiple—the basic stuff of creation—into the final unity of Christ who is one with God. In this context, Teilhard's plea for the unity of Christianity's essential mysteries cannot be called arbitrary. His effort to make this point is further motivated by his realization of the fact that "the old cosmos (static, limited, and open at every moment to rearrangement)" has been superseded by "the modern universe (organically welded by its space-time into a single evolutive whole)," and he believes accordingly that Christianity's self-understanding ought to reflect its understanding and appreciation of the universe in which it finds itself.[14]

It is hardly surprising if Teilhard's position on the unity of the Christian mysteries appears somewhat left of center when viewed from the perspective of traditional Christian teaching. Clearly, the points at issue are whether or not Teilhard's theory is compatible with God's freedom and transcendence in the creative process, and

whether or not his theory compromises the gratuity or gift-character of the present redemptive order. Perhaps a reconsideration of our ideas of transcendence and divine freedom will serve to assure us of Teilhard's basic continuity with theological tradition. Indeed, Teilhard himself opens the door to a deeper appreciation of God's involvement with creation when he suggests that in plumbing the depths of divine motivation, "our intelligence can no longer distinguish at all between supreme necessity and supreme freedom, except by recognizing the presence of the Free in the infallible sign of an accompanying love."[15]

In other words, as soon as creation is taken seriously as a work of divine love, any false alternative between freedom and necessity is precluded. Our argument may be fashioned in the following way. In God, there is never any question of the kind of physical necessity or mechanical determinism found within material processes where things happen inevitably as the result of a chain of causes. But among conscious beings there is often another kind of necessity, a personal and moral necessity arising from within the atmosphere of love. Granted that love is a free commitment, that commitment, once made, implies obligations and responsibilities. To meet these obligations is to insure the growth of love; to refuse them is to abandon love. The person in love has to show his affection; but he also proves his love in deeds because he wants to. Precisely on the human level it is difficult to establish a priority between having to love because one wants to, and wanting to love or show one's love because one has to. Somehow, within the phenomenon of love there is the experience of that paradoxical and liberating necessity in which the lover loses himself for his loved one only to find himself enriched.

Teilhard would have us allow God this same opportunity to love. If God is love, and if love is never tired of expressing itself, then there are infinite ways in which God's love may appear. It so happens that he chooses the creative process and all that it implies. He loves creation not because he needs it; rather he needs it because he loves it. Thus we can say that by loving creatively, God has freely chosen not to be absolutely self-sufficient. What he loves, and how he loves, are matters of importance to him, and his commitment to what he creates is ratified in the incarnation and redemption, and pledged to fulfillment at the Pleroma; in this way God fulfills his obligations contracted in love. But in all this he has not compromised himself; what he does, he does freely.

Thus the argument can be made that Teilhard's position rests on the fact that he takes the infinity of God seriously, and allows it to manifest itself in all its surprising richness. Jesus Christ, in his incarnation, is the self-expression of God as he spends himself in love. Through and in Christ the process of love is extended throughout the universe by means of the redemptive action accomplished in Christ's total immersion in matter by suffering and death, an immersion repeatedly realized in the symbol and sign of the Eucharist and the breaking of the Bread.[16] Because the generosity of God is total, the universe can rejoice in the promise of its own eventual transformation and completion. But when everything is done, it is Christ who is built up, and he returns everything to the Father (1 Cor. 3:23). Thus, also with God it is true that he who empties himself comes to fulfillment.

In affirming the transcendence of God, the crucial point is not that we maintain God's necessary and complete independence from creation. Rather, we must maintain that for all his dependence on creation, for all that he is in relation to creation, God is not identified with it, not confined or totally limited to it. Thus God's reality and meaning might be described as constituting both the ground and goal of all creation, so immanently involved with every being as to be the ultimate explanation of each one's power of self-transcendence—all this without in any way compromising the divine transcendence. This is the kind of transcendence suggested by Teilhard, a transcendence which preserves the unique identity of God even in the Pleroma, the age of fullness when all shall be one with God, a way of being which is "obtained not by identification (God becoming all) but by the differentiating and communicating action of love (God all in everyone). And that is essentially orthodox and Christian [1 Cor. 15:28] ."[17] In this way, then, we can perhaps credit Teilhard with having held in balance the infinity of God, his generosity and freedom, together with the essential necessity and importance which the universe now has in its relationship with God.

In concluding this section of our study we may fairly say that in Teilhard's world-view, Jesus Christ is taken out of the historical niche of two thousand years ago; he becomes trans-historical and thus equally necessary and important for all times. On the basis of revelation (Col. 1:15-17; Eph. 2:10; 1 Cor. 8:6), Teilhard argues that the concrete reality of Jesus Christ somehow pre-exists his incarnation and is in fact co-extensive and co-existent with all of

time and creation. In whatever sense, then, that creation and the creative process of God are eternal, in this same sense, at least, Christ is eternal. In explaining the pervasive influence of the pre-existent Christ in the universe, Teilhard suggests that in creating, God willed to have his Christ, but in order that Christ might be, there first had to be a world of the spirit, especially a human world; and in order for such a world to be, the process of organic life had to be initiated, and in order for this to occur, the creation of the cosmos was required.[18] Thus, to say that God willed Christ from the beginning of time is perhaps to say neither more nor less than that from the beginning of time he willed to incarnate his love, his goodness, and finally to unite to himself the creation and fruit of his love (1 Cor. 15: 20-28).

Evil, Sin and Redemption

It is in the light of Teilhard's theory of creative union that we must consider his views on evil, sin, and the specific meaning of the redemptive work of Jesus Christ. According to Faricy, Teilhard sees redemption mainly as a creative striving to achieve victory over the powers of evil. In turn, evil is understood as an incompleteness of organization in a creation that is progressing toward a higher state of unity. In an evolving universe, as Teilhard points out, "for implacable statistical reasons, and at every level—preliving, living, reflectively conscious—it is impossible that there not be some disorder or lack of organization in a multiplicity that is **progressively** moving toward a higher degree of organization."[19]

There is for Teilhard only one type of evil, namely, disunion, and we speak of moral evil only when this disunion affects the free zones of the soul, that is, when human beings freely decide to introduce disunity into the world. Human beings sin precisely when they refuse to be part of the movement toward the Omega point of evolution or when, in other words, they refuse to contribute to that fundamental energy of life-giving love which is indeed the bloodstream itself of spiritual evolution, and which alone can draw people together and bring them to their final end.[20] Teilhard is aware, however, that both the quantity and the intense malice of the evil which is spread throughout the world lend a dimension to humanity's rejection of love that, in the eyes of many, defies rational explanation. Teilhard is thus brought to consider whether, to the idea of evil as the normal effect or accompaniment of evolution, there must not be added the idea of evil as "the **extraordinary effect** of some catastrophe or primordial deviation." Here lies the question of original sin.[21]

Teilhard's consideration of the doctrine of original sin is strongly motivated by his sensitivity to the collapse of geocentrism. Given the Roman Catholic Church's traditional conviction that "evil (first moral, and then physical) entered the world as the result of a **fault** committed by an **individual human** being," the question must be squarely faced, says Teilhard, whether this explanation for the universal presence of evil, with the subsequent need for the all-encompassing redemptive action of Christ, may still logically be maintained once science has allowed the earth to reveal the true extent of the universe's temporal and spatial dimensions. In other words, Teilhard suggests that theology cannot pretend that the dethronement of humanity and its earth from the center of the universe is not a fact to be reckoned with. Granting the expanded horizons of the universe, Teilhard poses the dilemma now facing a believer in these terms: "either he must completely redraw the historical representation of original sin"—seen, that is, as a first and single man's disobedience—"or he must restrict the theological Fall and Redemption to a small portion of the universe that has reached such boundless dimensions."[22]

Driven by his undying faith in the complete centrality of Christ as the being "in whom all things hold together" (Col. 1:17), Teilhard is intent upon preserving the all-embracive universality of Christ's redemptive activity. To do this, however, he must recast theological interpretation and establish an original sin as vast as the universe, for otherwise Christ must be seen as having saved only a part of creation and would thus not truly be the center of all. It is for this reason that throughout his career Teilhard re-formulates the traditional doctrine of original sin in the most cosmic terms possible. He writes, for example, that taken in its widest sense, original sin "is not a malady specific to the earth, nor is it bound up with human generation." It represents, rather, the inevitable chance of evil that accompanies the existence of all created being. For Teilhard, original sin simply cannot be located at any one point in space and time; rather, it is everywhere, constituting "a general condition affecting the whole of history."[23]

Teilhard remains always deeply aware of the fact that the more the past is brought into clearer focus by means of scientific investigation, the less can we accommodate the idea of a single individual who is responsible for the universal plight of humanity. Consequently, Teilhard repudiates both the historicity and the individuality of "Adam," without infidelity, however,—and this must be emphasized —to the two essential tenets of the traditional doctrine of original sin, namely, the presence of sin in every human being, and the resultant necessity for universal redemption. There is, then, strictly speaking, no first Adam. This name simply disguises, says Teilhard, "a universal and unbreakable law of reversion or perversion—the price that has to be paid for progress." Adam symbolizes the fact that all people are marked by original sin, but not as a result of some aboriginal fault of a primitive human; rather, people find themselves in original sin because this is the law of the universe, a basic condition both of a world in evolution and of human beings in the process of becoming.[24]

Up to this point Teilhard has spoken of original sin in broad or general terms as the evil which inheres in the world as a natural expression of its method of creation. He is quite aware, however, that in the strict sense of the word, the original sin, which is the specific concern of theologians, occurs when this universal evil is definitely concretized in the lives of human beings gifted with freedom and called to responsible activity. In other words, Teilhard leaves room for a specifically human original sin but this is really no more than the actualization and assimilation of the "well-spring of sin" which has permeated the matter of the universe from the time of its creation.[25] One thing that is definitely called into question in Teilhard's understanding of humanity's original sin is its characterization as a Fall from some original state of perfection or justice. It is true, of course, that he uses the term "Fall" and that in his early writings he is willing to entertain the possibility of some paradisical state, provided it is understood in a non-historical or extra-historical and pre-cosmic sense. In later writings, however, Teilhard shows less sympathy or patience with the idea of original justice and is more courageous in arguing its accidental or extraneous relationship to the essence of the Christian doctrine of original sin. He always personally prefers to regard the perfection of the traditionally-depicted paradise as a representation of the salvation which is offered to all, but which may only be attained at some point in the future through the medium of unification in Christ.[26] The golden age of humanity lies not in the past, but in the future; it is not a faded memory; it is a vision of hope. The glory of the human race is, in short, seen by Teilhard as an eschatological rather than as a protological reality.

In his most mature reflections on the question of original sin, Teilhard offers an interpretation which involves two key elements: evolutive creation, and a statistical origin of evil.[27] He makes his proposal on the basis of what he sees as sound physical and theological reasons. Teilhard's initial postulate is that the only rational form of nothingness which could become the matter or material for the process of creation is radical multiplicity or what he calls "the multiple," non-being in its pure state. From this starting-point, creation is intelligible only as the gradual process of ordering and unifying the elements of the primordial multiple, which is not in any way directly sinful but which, in the process of being gradually organized and unified throughout the immensities of time and space, must, on the basis of statistics, necessarily endure error and disorder. As evolution progresses, the ordinary forces of disorganization and disorder manifest themselves in different ways: at the level of life, these forces entail suffering, and in human beings they take the shape of sin. It is significant that in Teilhard's proposal, the multiple, the source of statistical evil, is the functional equivalent of the first Adam. This tenet alone unties for Teilhard the Gordian knot of the problem of evil, for in this context physical suffering and moral transgression no longer stand in contradiction to either the power of God or his goodness. Rather, these realities appear simply as part of the very structure of created or participated being and in no way represent any deficiency in the creative act of God. They are, as Teilhard says, "the **statistically inevitable by-product** of the unification of the multiple."

In its cosmic dimensions, original sin is interpreted as an inherent part of the mechanism of creation; it represents, in fact, "the action of the negative forces of 'counter-evolution'."[28] As noted above, Teilhard sees in this explanation no infidelity to the two dogmatic requirements of the theology of original sin. First, Christ's redemption is still universal in that it remedies a situation—the ubiquitous presence of disorder—which accompanies the radical nature of a universe still in the process of being created. Secondly, each new human being bears the burden imposed by the accumulated influence of past, present and future transgressions. For Teilhard, there is no question but that his interpretation of original sin recognizes the basic demands both of modern science and of authentic Christianity.[29]

There is an interesting outcome to Teilhard's presentation of the Creation, Fall, Incarnation, and Redemption as universal, nonaccidental events that are co-extensive with the spatial-temporal dimensions of the world. For now, he asks, must we not look for the supreme transgression, not in the past when humanity was inarticulate, but rather in the future, "when mankind has at last become fully conscious of its powers and will split into two camps, for God or against him?"[30] With this change in perspective the attitude of humanity is also altered. No longer is our existence spent in the effort to make up for the past faults of humanity; the emphasis is put rather on a thrust into the future in such a way as to avoid the great sin of apostasy. Success in this undertaking is dependent upon our enduring association with the Christ whose power to overcome and to unify the disparate forces of creation is increasingly felt the more closely we approach him.

Several critical observations regarding Teilhard's theory of original sin are in order here. While no doubt can be cast upon the basic consistency in Teilhard's reflections upon original sin, it is evident that the idea of its involving some fall from an original state of justice and integrity comes to have less and less significance for him, the reason being, that he sees original sin as a non-isolable, trans-historical reality. The strict theological meaning of sin is preserved, however, in Teilhard's depiction of humanity's free appropriation and extension of the disunity rooted in the universe. And yet a strange reversal is revealed here, for in the traditional theological presentation of the origins of human history, moral evil is seen as preceding physical evil and as being its cause, whereas in Teilhard's theory physical evil precedes moral evil and prepares its way. Finally, if the reality of sin is preserved in Teilhard's theology, if, that is, humanity is responsible for sin's appearance in the world as moral evil, so also is the reality of redemption, along with its necessity and gratuity, preserved. But the redemption is now understood, as we shall see, in more positive terms, and its gratuity, that is, Christ's free involvement with, and concern for, creation, is best understood as an expression of the freedom of love which, once offered, finds itself necessarily bound to spend and extend itself in order to preserve fidelity to its commitment.

Teilhard's movement away from the doctrine of "the Fall" and his development of a theology of positive redemption are obvious outgrowths of his theology of creation which, in turn, is shaped by two major factors: his undying vision of the centrality of Jesus Christ and his unyielding conviction that the traditional Christian teachings regarding creation offer only a static solution to the problem of evil. They try, that is, to explain the presence of evil in a fixed universe. Quite logically, in a universe which supposedly issues fully formed from the hand of God, disorder can ultimately result only from some kind of secondary or subsequent distortion. But if, as Teilhard maintains, the universe is even now still in the process of being creatively transformed by God, and is thus only gradually emerging from a multiplicity of matter toward a unity of spirit, then there is no longer any need to postulate a primordial mishap, a Fall, as an explanation, either of the various multiples, dualities, and disunities so apparent in our experience of the world, or of this multiplicity's satellite, evil.[31]

In a processive world, moreover, where evil expresses the state of plurality that is only incompletely organized, it must be expected that its transitory state of imperfection will find expression eventually in culpable acts, the first examples of which, while they may be least conscious, are still most decisive for human history and thus may be regarded as giving expression to a "primary transgression." For Teilhard, however, the original weakness to which creation is subject is really its radical origin in the multiple. Thus, whatever else evil finally is, it is not an unforeseen accident in the history of the universe. On the contrary, Teilhard has this to say of evil:

> It is an enemy, a shadow which God inevitably produces simply by the fact that he decides on creation. New being, launched into existence and not yet completely assimilated into unity, is a dangerous thing, bringing with it pain and oddity. For the Almighty, therefore, to create is no small matter: it is no picnic, but an adventure, a risk, a battle to which he commits himself unreservedly.[32]

It is in this context that Teilhard presents his theology of positive redemption. Christ becomes the incarnation of the Father's love and yearning for the victory of creation. In himself, and for all of us, Christ overcomes the resistance which the primordial multiplicity offers to unification and which matter shows toward the rise of spirit. Truly, Christ "is the symbol and the sign-in-action of progress. The complete and definitive meaning of redemption is **no longer only** to expiate: it is to surmount and conquer."[33] Redemption, then, like creation, belongs to the category of "effort." Without ceasing to be the one who bears the sins of the world, Christ the Redeemer becomes more and more Christ the Evolver, the one "who bears and supports the weight of the world in evolution." For Teilhard, it is simply essential that in a universe which is in the process of being unified, the Cross, if it is to reign over the earth, must present itself as a sign not simply of expiation for sin, but more so of the progress toward God resulting from Christ's breakthrough into history. Moreover, since humanity's union with God, the goal of the creative and redemptive process, presupposes and demands our co-operation with God's creative will and our participation in his creative action, the redemptive value of Christ's incarnation grants no dispensation which would excuse us from resisting evil with all our strength.[34]

The laborious process of unification is long but it is infinitely encouraged and facilitated by the incarnation of God's Word, his "Yes" to creation. Jesus Christ makes clear the seriousness of God's good will toward creation, and this on several levels. By entering into the multiplicity of matter, Christ has offset the basic inertia of disorganization. Within the material universe there is still the hesitancy, disorder, and failure of physical evil; there is still the moral evil of hatred and injustice among people, but fundamentally the movement of creation toward unification and fulfillment in Christ and finally in God has been advanced. Final success has been hastened and guaranteed through Christ's redemptive action, the positive meaning of which is the support given by his life, suffering, death, and resurrection to the upward and forward movement of humanity.

Given the nature of man as a personal, self-conscious being, Teilhard is convinced that the only goal or consummation of human history which is satisfactory for man is a personalized one like love, which brings the human personality to fulfillment without stagnation. Moved by these rational considerations of the goal of humanity, on one hand, and by his religious convictions, on the other, Teilhard comes to identify the Omega point, the climax of the evolutionary process, with the Christ of revelation. Thus the Redeemer becomes the Christ-Omega, the cosmic-Christ, the super-Christ, the universal Christ, Christ the Evolver who "saves the world in the sense that without Christ . . . man's effort would be without hope in a final outcome, and this would mean his losing the taste for life and abandoning altogether his task on earth."[35] To become the effective redeeming hope of the universe in its struggle for fulfillment, Christ had to become an immanent part of the process. Moreover, he had to experience the full force of the powers of disorder at work within this process. All this he did through his "kenosis into matter" in his birth, life, suffering, and death.

It seems quite legitimate, then, to view Christ chiefly as Evolver and thus to stress the primary elevating, unitive, and fulfilling aspect of redemption. But there is always the secondary or reparative dimension to Christ's work, whereby the forces of evil, regression, and dispersion are overcome. As was seen above, Teilhard pictures moral evil or sin as an individual's refusal to love. In this context, evolution is properly perceived as a movement threatened "from within by a weakness inherent in man, its crowning achievement, namely the fragility of human love and freedom." Sin alone can wipe out the hope of progress toward the Christ-Omega. If evolution is to be victorious, and if humanity is to have a future which it can enjoy, there must first be a victory over sin. Christ's own love provides this victory and his work of reparation is the strengthening of human love, the impetus given to people to turn from their refusal of love.[36]

Thus there is an immense irony in Teilhard's thinking: with regard to the future of man, human love is the source both of ambiguity and of encouragement with respect to the completion of Christ's redemptive activity; depending on the reality and seriousness of our commitment to loving our neighbors, we can hamper or assist the workings of God. This means that the only certain guarantee of evolution's success is Christ's effective conquest of our capacity for disunion and hatred. In Teilhard's thinking about the redemptive role of Christ, humanity is still in the process of being born in Christ without whose appearance among us we were not helpless, but only hopeless. Without hope and the dignity it instills, without hope and the conviction it inspires that the future belongs to us, our lot was indeed unenviable. It is from this dire predicament, however, that we have been rescued by Christ who gives flesh to the promise of the future that has been freely offered by the Father and is available to us on the condition that we help prepare the way for it by building the world in love.

The Function of Morality: Constructing the Earth

As was suggested earlier, Teilhard sees the significance of Christian life precisely in its perpetuation of the two aspects of Christ's redemptive work. In line with the creative aspect of Christ's work, the Christian labors in a conquest of the world through love, while at the same time in the continuation of the work of reparation and expiation, the Christian is called to a renunciation of the world. But both aspects of Christian living must be seen always as two dimensions of one tendency: to be united with God in and through the world. The Christian brings this tendency to life in the daily efforts to build the world in view of the eschaton.[37]

It is in this context that Teilhard outlines what he calls an "ethics of movement or of conquest," which goes beyond what he sees as the usual "ethics of balance or of equilibrium," understood as a fixed system of rights and duties aimed at establishing and maintaining a static equilibrium among individuals or societies. In the past, moral standards have been designed largely to protect individuals and society mainly by means of a limitation of energies or a restraint of forces. The premise upon which this traditional morality is based is that every individual or society is an absolute term whose autonomy must be protected. But it is precisely such a premise which an evolutionary scheme calls into question, for the real concern now is not so much to protect individuals and safeguard their rights, but rather to guide them to personal fulfillment within a human community, and indeed on behalf of that community.

In the dynamic morality envisioned by Teilhard, the highest good is that which seeks the best development of the person, of society, and of the world. Thus he claims that whereas formerly the aim of ethics was to protect, now it is to develop; no longer is the ethicist a kind of lawyer or tight-rope walker; he is becoming "the technician and engineer of the spiritual energies of the world."[38] Because evolution has achieved reflective consciousness in humanity, it now recognizes to some degree its place in the world and can thus choose its direction or withhold its efforts; consequently, the problem of action becomes crucial. In a statically conceived universe, says Teilhard, the origin of duty might variously be explained on the basis of an explicit command issued by a totally extrinsic source, or recourse might be had to an irrational but categorical instinct. In a spiritually evolutionary scheme, however, an individual's duty is established differently; it rests upon the fact that each of us is born and develops **as a function of a cosmic stream**, so that we must act, and we must act in a certain way, "because our individual destinies are dependent on a universal destiny."[39]

63

What are the implications of this rather enigmatic view? Teilhard acknowledges that the function of morality is to construct the world, and he presents three general principles of his ethics of conquest. The first principle states that **only** that which "makes for the growth of the spirit on earth" is finally good. In light of this principle it must be said that whereas in the past an individual could live his life as he wished provided he infringed on no one else's rights, now no use of life or personal talents is morally acceptable unless that use is somehow in the service of humanity. Thus, for example, concerning money and other material possessions, Teilhard maintains that the morality of such riches is determined by the extent to which "they **work** for the benefit of the spirit."[40]

In the second principle Teilhard claims that "**everything** that brings a spiritual growth to the world" is at least basically and partially good. The effect of this principle is to introduce the element of risk into Christian living; there is no place for timidity or for "playing it safe." Because the morality of balance was satisfied simply with the maintenance of an order which kept the machinery of humanity from grinding and overheating, it could avoid taking the trouble of finding out whether or not real spiritual possibilities were being excluded from the system it had constructed. No longer is such an attitude tolerable, however.

Finally, Teilhard's third principle argues that what is ultimately **best** is what assures the spiritual powers of the earth their highest development. On the basis of the premise that the universe is in a state of spiritual transformation, the human obligation is to move everything in the direction of the greatest consciousness, that is, as we shall see, in the direction of love. It follows, then, that the general and highest law of morality is this: "to limit force (unless for the purpose of obtaining even more force) **is sin**." Teilhard's meaning here is that limiting the energy or force of love is sin unless, of course, the intention of such limiting is to create more love.

For Teilhard, the morality of balance appears as a closed morality in which "a minimum of internal frictions in a regulated state is both the ideal to which it tends and a sign that it has reached it." By contrast, the morality of conquest, as an open morality, can only be defined by its relationship to a state or object still to be reached, which means that this goal must "shine with enough light to be desired and held in view." Thus, while the morality of balance

64

may logically be agnostic and engrossed in possessing the present moment, a morality of conquest inclines by necessity toward the future in pursuit of a God, who not only assists in the unification of humanity by a spiritual transformation of the forces of matter, but also assures that this reconciliation renders ever more distinguishable and unique those who lose themselves in him and for him. Teilhard's vision, then, is clearly broad enough to encompass "a universal God to be realized by effort, and yet a personal God to be submitted to in love." At one and the same time, God confronts humanity with a call to labor and a freedom to respond with an energy and a hope beyond that warranted by the present empirical situation itself; the abiding condition for progress is, however, that the demands of love be recognized, weighed and met.

Teilhard accepts Julian Huxley's description of humanity as "nothing else than evolution become conscious of itself." No longer is humanity seen as the center of the universe; rather, it is "something more wonderful—the arrow pointing the way to the final unification of the world in terms of life." But here a problem arises, for once evolution becomes conscious of itself in human beings, once it is gifted with foresight, then it moves forward only on the condition that its way is not blocked, that it sees ahead of itself a suitable outcome. Thus either an opening to fulfillment exists for the evolutionary process or else creation is closed to the demands of futurity, in which case the universe is self-abortive and absurd. There are only two alternatives: absolute optimism or absolute pessimism; human beings either move upward toward union or downward toward disorganization. Teilhard concludes that while there is no irrefutable tangible evidence for either side, "in support of hope, there are rational invitations to an act of faith."[41] Up to this point, then, Teilhard's ethic is a call for the future development of both the personal and social dimensions of human existence; it is also a call for the development of the world through the mediation and influence of human activity. But both the impetus to this development and the continuing assurance of human involvement in it rest upon humanity's hope in Christ for its final success.

Love: The Law of Socialization and Personalization

Central to Teilhard's thesis regarding the building both of the human race and of the human world, is his recognition that humanity concretely is composed of different branches, each having value precisely in its diversity. Such diversity may manifest itself in functional differences and inequalities when viewed within the process of unification, but from the viewpoint of "**their essential complementarity**" these differences and inequalities become "acceptable, honorable, and even welcome." From this suggestion of functional diversity, Teilhard draws two conclusions: first, that each of these branches of humanity must use its own qualities and genius to complete and fulfill itself in the future, and secondly, that in this push for fulfillment, help must be sought from neighboring branches. In their mutual assistance the human branches must replace exploitation, suppression, and hostile competition—all of which are found among subhuman zoological groups—with neighborly emulation. The law of the jungle must yield to the law of teamwork; war has no sense except in relation to dangers or conquests outside humanity. As Teilhard sees the human situation, then, we must leave "the age of nations" behind us; our present task, if we do not want to perish, is "to shake off ancient prejudices, and to build the earth."[42]

It is Teilhard's opinion that in the struggle for human fulfillment, we can no longer rely solely on the mechanical laws of natural selection as these apply within the human field. For too long we have simply bowed to "the so-called infallibility of nature" and allowed humanity to develop at random. At some point in the future it is indispensable, says Teilhard, that we turn our attention toward discovering and developing a "nobly human form of eugenics, on a standard worthy of our personalities . . ." We must, in addition, create a science of "human energetics" which would concern itself with geo-economics, geo-politics, and geo-demography; it would face issues, for example, like the distribution of the world's resources, the movement of people into the earth's unpopulated regions, and the best use of the forces set free by mechanization.[43]

Teilhard realizes that this type of thinking gives rise to many fears and uncertainties. He is aware of the fact that in every human heart a conflict can arise between the individual, who grows ever more conscious of his or her individual worth, and social affiliations whose demands become ever more pressing. But at the same time Teilhard is convinced that this conflict is one of appearance only. As he sees it, collectivization and individualization are not at odds but constitute, rather, two expressions of the single process of socialization which signals not the end of the era of the individual, but much more its beginning.

In order to understand Teilhard's thinking on this point, we must be aware of the distinction he sees between human individuality and human personhood. For Teilhard, the apex of human originality lies not in our individuality but in our personhood, which, in an evolutionary world, we can only find by uniting together with others. "The true ego grows in inverse proportion to 'egoism'." Thus to seek to individualize ourselves, in the sense of separating ourselves as much as possible from others, is to become retrograde; to insist on individual autonomy in isolation from others is to seek "to drag the world backwards towards plurality and into matter."[44] Although Teilhard in no way sanctions society running roughshod over the individual person, he nonetheless suggests, when drawing up a declaration on human rights, that we should no longer strive "to organize the world in favor of, and in terms of, the isolated individual;" instead we should attempt "to combine all things for the perfection ('personalization') of the individual by his well-ordered integration with the unified group in which Mankind must eventually culminate, both organically and spiritually."[45]

In a context like this it is clear that a definition of individual human rights admits of no simple formulation. Nevertheless, as a minimal requirement for such a definition, Teilhard proposes that with respect to the individual we must recognize three facts: the individual has an absolute duty, a relative right, and an absolute right. Or it can be said that there are three principles which must be incarnated and find expression in the building of the earth. (1) The individual has an absolute duty to develop his or her own personality because the perfection of our neighbors depends upon our own individual perfection. (2) It is "the relative right of the individual to be placed in circumstances as favorable as possible to his personal development." The relative nature of this claim is explained by the fact that society, for its own sake, must concern itself with creating "the most favorable environment for the full development (physical and spiritual) of what is special" to each individual. Thus an investigation into, and evaluation of, each person's situation is called for. (3) Within society it is the individual's absolute right not to be crushed by external coercion; the individual may be subjected, however, to persuasion which is "in conformity with his personal endowments and aspirations." Finally, in conjunction with this principle Teilhard insists that never must the powers of society be allowed to force the individual "to deform or falsify himself."[46]

Having looked at the general aim of Teilhard's ethics, we must now ask how he envisions this goal being achieved. It is easily seen that for Teilhard the future is built, the movement involving the growth of spirit takes place, and finally unification is achieved, only by means of the operative principle of love, that basic form of energy which maintains the process of cosmogenesis. The world is built up, the future is prepared, precisely in and through the activity of love, and only to the extent that humanity labors to realize the union of love can we be said to contribute to the development of the spiritual powers of the earth. Within Teilhard's evolutionary scheme, love alone can unite "living beings in such a way as to complete and fulfill them, for it alone takes them and joins them by what is deepest in themselves . . ." Love, in other words, presents itself as truly a union which differentiates, which preserves and fosters the values and separate identities of those who commit themselves to it. On this basis, Teilhard can suggest that a universal love is not only psychologically possible, but also "it is the only complete and final way in which we are able to love."[47]

It is at this point that the data of Christian revelation again have their impact upon Teilhard's thinking, for he presents Christ as Alpha and Omega, the beginning and end, the one in whom the whole universe is personalized. When Teilhard speaks of Christ as the term and motive force of evolution, when, in fact, he characterizes Christ as the Evolver, he intends to affirm that Christ is attainable in and through the whole process of evolution. Cosmogenesis, through the media of biogenesis, anthropogenesis and noogenesis, is actually expressive of Christogenesis, so that the whole of reality is charged with a divine Presence. Teilhard sees Christ as the cosmic-Christ under whose influence our charity is universalized, energized, and synthesized. "Everything becomes physically and literally lovable in God, and God, in return, becomes intelligible and lovable in everything around us." Thus, in a world filled by God, universal communion becomes for the first time a real possibility.

Regarding the role of Christ in energizing and synthesizing the force of love, Teilhard remarks that there was a time when the love of God seemed to involve no more than an attitude of contemplation, whereby people attempted to rise above human distractions and passions in order to find rest and comfort in the warm sun of the divine countenance. In the area of human relationships, Christians too often interpreted love of neighbor simply as the effort to bind up the wounds of their fellow human beings and thus to alleviate their sufferings. But in the process of Christogenesis things are otherwise. Where Christ can be attained fully only at the term and peak of cosmic evolution, detachment and pity—simply escaping from the world and mitigating evil—are clearly revealed in their inadequacy as marks of Christian charity. The love of God and of our neighbors must now involve the Christian in a positive movement toward Christ whereby the Christian attempts to complete and synthesize everything in him.

In the presence of Christ the Evolver, and under the power of this universal Christ, the infinite modalities of human action are fused into a single form—that of love—just as the countless shades of color combine in nature to produce a single white light. In this divine milieu, every action, as Teilhard says, is "amorized." Now every action, to the extent that it is directed toward Christ, takes on, without any change in its own nature, the character of an act of love.[48] The energy of love is thus transformed into Christian charity, that vibrant milieu embracing and superanimating all the forces of the earth. The Christian life, rooted in faith and shaped by hope, comes to be lived and spent in love. What Teilhard does, however, is to stress the other side of the biblical truth that we cannot love God without loving our neighbor; his emphasis is on the fact that we cannot love our neighbor without drawing closer to God.[49]

What can be expected in a universe on its way to unification in Christ? Teilhard is convinced that in just such a world, suffering is both natural and necessary. "Nothing is more beatific than union attained; nothing more laborious than the pursuit of union." There are three reasons why a personalizing evolution is necessarily painful for human beings: such an evolution "is basically a plurality; it advances by differentiation; it leads to metamorphoses." Teilhard's intention here is to stress his understanding that unification is a labor, that advances in personalization must be paid for with pain and suffering, and that any enterprise, still unfinished, must invariably suffer the disorder resulting from its residual plurality and lack of organization. Finally, in the process of self-integration and of unification with others, human beings cannot avoid those critical points of stress which prohibit growth unless it is paid for through renunciation and transformation. Yet in the midst of this present struggle and its anguish, there is some compensation, which consists, Teilhard claims, in the joy that springs from the faith and hope that indeed the birth of a personalized universe began long ago. This brings us to the heart of Christianity: it is nothing more nor less than "a belief in the unification of the world in God by the Incarnation."[50]

The struggle to enhance the personalization of the universe gives shape to Teilhard's dynamic morality of conquest. Cooperation with Christ in the work of unification manifests itself in Christian living on three levels. Putting it another way, there are three crucial virtues, each operating to effect unification on a different level: purity, charity, and self-denial. Through purity, the individual attains a certain self-possession, a concentration of energies, which may then be channeled into the work of charity in order to effect a basic unity among people; and finally, in self-denial is accomplished the re-orientation of all people from themselves toward Christ, and thus toward God.[51] It is essential for Teilhard's thinking, however, that detachment and self-denial be seen as positive realities. Christians are detached because of their commitment to Christian action. Their whole life-style is patterned on the Incarnation—immersion in the world so as to lead the world to God. Mortification and ascetic discipline have meaning only in the plan of love. There is value in pain when there is suffering with a purpose, or where there is love.

Today's Christians find significance only in a spiritual detachment which turns their interest outward to the good of others. When they are engaged in the work of love, when they are contributing their share to the re-creation of the universe by "restoring all things in Christ," then Christians are truly forgetful of themselves. They are beside themselves with love. With asceticism, self-denial, and love hand-in-hand, Christians make of themselves instruments of God's charity. They grow in themselves and in their neighbors, but always and ultimately in Christ and toward God. Thus, detachment from self derives its meaning, and even its strength, from attachment to Christ and to his creation, which means that the whole inclination of asceticism is toward affirmation: "To be fully human and fully alive, a man must first be centered on himself [purity], then centered away from himself in others [charity] and finally centered beyond himself in Someone greater than he [self-denial]."[52]

For the Christian who is dedicated to the unification of the world in Christ, the entire task of the interior moral life is reduced to the two essential and complementary processes of attachment and detachment: "to conquer the world, and to escape from it," at least as it now presents itself; together, these processes represent two forms of one and the same urge: "to come together with God through the world." Because the material and spiritual development of the universe is ultimately directed through Christ toward the Father, Christians have the happiness of knowing that Christ is waiting to receive the fruit of their labor.

What is important now is not simply the intention behind the action but also the tangible results of the work. In this way Christians are inspired in their efforts to conquer the world. This is a task, however, which calls at the same time for a basic detachment from the present form of the world that, like humanity, is involved in an ascent that is a true way of the cross. Under the inexorable necessity to grow greater and to achieve both an inner personal center and a communal unity, humanity and the universe evolve through successive metamorphoses in which the outer shells of the old forms, the old self, are continually sloughed off. Christians who are striving for an interior purification and integration may delight in knowing that in this way they are engaged all the while in an active effort to grow greater for Christ. Teilhard hastens to assure us, moreover, that the joy of Christians is itself a passivity at least in this respect, that "it is Christ himself, in the very depths of our being, who seeks to be born and grow greater in our bodies and souls."[53]

In the end, the most magnificent of the prerogatives of the Universal Christ is his power to be operative in humanity, not only through the natural impulses of life, but also in the jarring events of defeat and death. But Christians must appreciate that transformation in Christ is effected neither immediately nor without their co-operation. Thus Teilhard keenly realizes the fact that we do not find God indiscriminately in the trials, sufferings and tribulations of life—"but solely **at the point of balance** between our desperate efforts to grow greater and the resistance to our domination that we meet from outside." Recourse to such terminology as "the point of balance" seems to indicate Teilhard's awareness that efforts at reaching, maintaining, and furthering an adequate individual ethic—and, **a fortiori**, an acceptable social ethic—demand a constant straining, a point of tension, where the decision must be made whether personal and collective humanization through the unification of the earth calls here and now for the positive action of conquest or for the negative action of suffering or detachment.

Teilhard's insistence would simply be that as agents of reconciliation and of unifying love, Christians are, and must be, effective in both ways. "**If we are to succeed in submitting ourselves to the will of God, we must first make a very great effort.**" The process of spiritualization and unification, which brings the universe out of a past of matter and multiplicity into a future of spirit and unity, always lies under the aegis of Christ the Victor who promises and guarantees an ultimate victory, but who also, because he remains the Crucified One, reminds us that the world is built in time only through struggle and failure, and the continually renewed efforts at growth.[54] Teilhard believes that if we do not learn to love, to transform the power of hate into the power of Christian charity, the world will explode. Nonetheless, Teilhard is convinced that such a transformation can and will occur because of the attraction exercised by Christ, the Omega—autonomous, actual, irreversible and transcendent.[55]

The Presence of Hope as the Possibility for Love

Teilhard offers an ethic and spirituality which are thoroughly contemporary and authentically Christian. He encourages the human desire to find God in material creation, and indeed in all things. He knows too that it is foolishness for Christians to seek or to expect any growth in personal fulfillment without the ingredients of pain and suffering, embraced and endured under the shadow of the Cross. And finally, Teilhard appreciates the human need to feel that the present is more than simply a single moment in a processive movement toward the future. While essentially involved in process, the present must somehow transcend change by means of its own intrinsic value, which it in fact has, according to Teilhard, precisely insofar as it embodies and is embraced by the dimension of Christian charity. The role of charity in Teilhard's theological reflection is thus crucial.[56]

Acknowledgment of the need for charity raises another question, however. If in the Teilhardian scheme of reality all creation is in and for Christ, and if the human task is to build up the universe, how, then, may we define humanity's role in the creation of the future? In answer to this question Teilhard uses imagery which portrays human achievement throughout history as a "preliminary sketch" or "rough draft" which is finally transfigured by God at the inauguration of the Parousia when the full glory of his kingdom is established. But the influence and initiative of God is not limited only to the final transformation of the work undertaken by human beings. Rather, God is active at every stage of man's making of himself and of his world, inviting and encouraging continued human involvement.

The Parousia, then, is simply the transformation of the whole of history into final glory, but all the while Christians are guided by the summoning presence of God in Christ into a future that is often terrifying in its newness and disheartening in its uncertainty. Since their involvement in building up the world is expected and needed, Christians see their contribution to the future as truly a creative one; yet, for Teilhard, as for St. Paul, the Christ of the Omega is also the Christ of the Alpha, so that all developments and progress take place in him and with him, in response to his invitation, and in co-operation with his grace. Throughout the process, moreover, it is the joyful hope of Christians in their creative response which serves as an inviting call to Christ for him to return once again, this time in all his glory.[57] In the following chapters we shall consider further this question of the contribution which Christians can make to the future of the world and to the appearance of God's kingdom. We shall be especially interested in seeing how Teilhard's thinking on these issues compares to that of Moltmann.

In light of Teilhard's own insistence upon love as the basic energy of the universe and as the only force effective both for the fulfillment of the individual and for the socialization of all human beings, the attempt to describe his ethical sketch as anything other than a morality of love might seem misguided.[58] And yet it is necessary to ask if there is not another overarching rubric which is needed to explain the general movement of Teilhard's theology, and hence of his ethical reflections. I suggest that there is indeed such a rubric: it is the experience of faith-inspired hope which serves to explain the varied balances in Teilhard's theological structure. Moreover, these are balances, it should be noted, which bear a striking resemblance to those which mark the experience of hope as explored in the previous chapter.

In Teilhard's eyes, hope for the future is what enables Christians to work in the present. Furthermore, it is both the prerogative and duty of Christians to unite their hope in Christ with their hope in humanity and in the world. Teilhard feels strongly that the expectation of an "issue" for the world, that is, a "way out" to its fulfillment, should be perhaps the most distinctive characteristic of

Christianity. Not surprisingly, he is unafraid to proclaim that Christ will only return if we earnestly expect him. And so Teilhard pleads for the appearance of Christians who are "as passionately vowed . . . to spreading the hopes of the Incarnation as are many humanitarians to spreading the dream of the new city."[59]

Teilhard labored to revive in the world this flame of Christian hope which burned so brightly in his own life. He was always aware that success in his effort would necessitate an increase among people of their interest "in the preparation and consummation of the Parousia." Such an interest, however, can be derived only "from the perception of **a more intimate connection** between the victory of Christ and the outcome of the work which our human effort here below is seeking to construct." This means, in effect, that in order to remain alive, the expectation of heaven must be incarnated in "a huge and totally human hope." Nor need Christians fear that in recognizing and proclaiming their hope for this world, they are merely placing their trust in an idol; rather, the more they succeed in building up the earth and in uniting humanity through an appreciation and mastery of its potentialities, "the more beautiful creation will be, . . . and the more Christ will find . . . a body worthy of resurrection." Teilhard argues that just as a circumference cannot have two centers, so also can the world not have two summits. Thus, "the star for which the world is waiting . . . is, necessarily, Christ himself in whom we hope," and so, "to desire the Parousia, all we have to do is to let the very heart of the earth, as we christianise it, beat within us."[60]

The vision of Teilhard reveals to him that the true Christian attitude is "**nihil intentatum**," "nothing untried." We must simply hope everything in and for Christ, and attempt everything in and for him, because "we shall never know all that the Incarnation still expects of the world's potentialities," nor shall we ever "put enough hope in the growing unity of mankind." No longer, then, ought we fear the temptations of a world, too large, nor the seductions of an earth, too beautiful, for these do not exist. Caught up in his vision of Christ, Teilhard proclaims in the end that the earth is in truth the divine milieu, the body of Christ, the one who is and who is coming.[61] In this overall context, then, the theological ethics proposed by Teilhard is best understood as one which is based upon a faith-inspired hope and built by love. Its goal is the unification of human beings with each other, with the world, and finally with God. But this unification is developed and strengthened only by a love which is rendered secure in the foundations of hope, for, as Teilhard puts it, "all conscious energy is, like love (and because it is love), founded on hope."[62]

There is in Teilhard's theology, moreover, no room for evolutionary determinism, for the process of evolution, as he understands it, is one which "**charges itself with an evergrowing measure of freedom.**" Because life is a movement of ceaseless discovery, there is thus a real sense in which the future belongs to those who, in a spirit of adventure, clearly and freely want to move ahead and are filled with the hope that they can do so. But more than the hope of adventure must motivate humanity. Teilhard is the first to acknowledge that the only movement which is for our good is the one which leads upward precisely by pushing forward, through ever-increasing organization, "to greater synthesis and unity."

The moral disposition, then, for growth into the future is this: "**a great hope held in common.**" And in this recognition, Teilhard parts company with committed individualists whom he sees as "egoists who seek to grow by excluding or diminishing their fellows, individually, nationally or racially." For Teilhard, there is no doubt but that, by its own growth in numbers and in relationships of mutual dependency, and by the very structure of the earth, humanity is being compelled by external forces to move toward greater unity. But the properly human task is to transform this external unifying power into an internal one, for only unification through unanimity can bring about the miracle whereby the forces of collectivity give birth to heightened personality.[63] It is in recognition of the communality of hope that the believer is moved to respect all the others to whom the new future has been promised. This respect, in turn, gives rise to a spirit of moderation which keeps the Christian from the excesses, either of running roughshod over the legitimate ambitions and aspirations of others, or of prescinding from their concerns in an attitude of false expectations regarding the workings of God.

Summary Reflections

In this brief concluding section some of the main points of Teilhard's thinking are recalled in an effort to show the organic unity of his work. Once the mysteries of creation, incarnation, and redemption are appreciated no longer simply as facts localized in space and time, but rather as true dimensions of the entire universe, Christian living is vitally transfigured. Now there is the expectation that the fulfillment of the redemption will be accomplished only in the convergence of the entire universe. Insofar as there has not occurred that conscious assimilation and integration of all things into the unique experience of Christ, the redemption is incomplete and, to this extent, awaits and demands the active co-operation of human beings. It is at this point that Christian ethics manifests its significance and function: Christian ethical living is participation in, and continuation of, the redemptive work of Christ, understood in both its unitive and reparative senses.

In Teilhard's thinking, Christians are called to reach heaven precisely by building up the earth. We seek God in all that we do, and in this way all that we do has value. In the Christian response of faith to the graciousness of God's incarnation, every action and task has eternal significance in itself. We are called to a dynamic morality of conquest, a pursuit of God, a spirituality of union with God in and through the world. It is clear by now that Teilhard cannot be satisfied with a morality of intention; he sees it as simply inadequate to say that human action has no value other than the intention which directs it. At the same time, he does not write off the importance of our intention. If we act in the Christian spirit, if we see with the eyes of faith, then everything we do is capable of becoming good (Rom. 8:28); there is value in both our attitude and labor, as well as in our accomplishments and finished tasks.

Teilhard objects to the juridical mentality which seeks to characterize our obligation to be engaged in building up the earth as "an obedience due to the more or less extrinsic and arbitrary order of a master." He cannot accept the view that the sole reason why we have to work is to give evidence of our good will, for in this theory what counts is clearly not the physical results of our labor, but rather the obedience we show in making things that are useless. Against this mentality Teilhard argues that we are expected and called on to produce more than "a fragile vessel, soon to crumble into powder." Precisely because Christ is the Omega-point of creation, nothing is foreign to the "physical building up of his universal body." Christ truly is waiting to receive the fruits of our work, and that includes not only the good intention behind our activity, but also the tangible results of our labors.[64] We are assured, moreover, that we can indeed have something of value to offer Christ, the Omega, because, as Alpha, he is already strengthening, freeing and guiding us in our labors.

For Teilhard, the pursuit of God ought not deflect Christians from human duties and human ends. Rather, in the Christian spirit we make our way to God in and through all human works. "God is inexhaustibly attainable in the totality of our action," but notice Teilhard says only that God is attainable; he does not say that God is automatically attained by an action whatsoever.[65] As Christians we must always look to the character of our activity. Our concern must be with the likelihood that our action will further the growth of spirit and give impetus to the process of greater unification. In other words, does our activity embody love? This is the final criterion. The answer to this question will not always—or even usually, perhaps—be easy; nor will our decision be facile. But Teilhard will not allow us to be satisfied with the status quo.

Morality is not conformity. Neither is it chaos. But in Teilhard's thinking these are not the only alternatives. We are called to engage in a morality of conquest that is based, not on any naturalistic optimism, but on the experience of Christian hope, which signifies that both our vision and our labor are taking shape under the light of the promised eschaton. Recognizing the availability of the new future, and intent upon achieving it, we strive to take rational and intelligent account of the facts of our situation in the world. These facts, however, must be seen finally not only as "occasions for resignation" but as "challenges to our intelligent love." The world as it is must yield to the world as it yet may become, a world fully fashioned in and by love. In the final analysis, then, Teilhard espouses a dynamic morality of conquest through creative responsibility, by means of which we give answer to God who desires an ever fuller presence in the creation he is committed to in love.[66] But as Teilhard understood so well, we respond as we should and God's presence among us is increased, only insofar as we spend ourselves in love.

Teilhard knows as well, however, that the day of the Lord, the new time, has already begun, and that we are to act accordingly. His thinking clearly embodies the fundamental dialogical character of all Christian life and reflection which is begun and continued through our response of faith in a self-revealing God who promises the eventual and final fulfillment of our hope, if only we can walk the path of present frustrations and disillusionments. Indeed, even as we walk this path, God opens up history and invites us to come ahead to receive in full the gift of his life; but enjoyment of this gift remains contingent upon our co-operative association with God as manifested in our participation in a dynamic morality of conquest. Precisely because we know in faith that we are not alone in our labors, and because our hope assures us that our labors are not in vain, we are encouraged and assisted in our strivings to love and thus to fulfill the conditions—necessary but, in themselves, not sufficient— for the return of our Lord in the fullness of his glory.

CHAPTER III

REFERENCES

1. Robert L. Faricy, S.J., Teilhard de Chardin's Theology of the Christian in the World (New York: Sheed & Ward, 1967), p. 26. The same point is made by N.M. Wildiers in his Foreword to Pierre Teilhard de Chardin, Christianity and Evolution, trans. René Hague (New York: Harcourt Brace Jovanovich, Inc., 1971) pp. 9-13.

2. Pierre Teilhard de Chardin, The Future of Man, trans. Norman Denny (New York: Harper Torchbooks, 1969), pp. 275-78.

3. Pierre Teilhard de Chardin, "Trois choses que je vois," pp. 4-5; an essay cited by Christopher F. Mooney, S.J., The Making of Man. Essays in the Christian Spirit (New York: Paulist Press, 1971), p. 161.

4. Teilhard in a letter cited by Claude Cuénot, "Teilhard et le Marxisme," Europe (March-April, 1965), p. 24, and quoted by Mooney, loc. cit. In a slightly modified form the sentence appears as a headline to Teilhard's essay "The Heart of the Matter," Future of Man, p. 272.

5. Teilhard, Future of Man, p. 280.

6. Ibid., pp. 281-82 and n. 5.

7. Pierre Teilhard de Chardin, The Phenomenon of Man, trans. Bernard Wall (New York: Harper Torchbooks, 2nd ed., 1965), p. 270; also his "Esquisse d'une dialectique de l'esprit," Activation de l'energie (Paris, 1963), p. 152 as cited by Mooney, Making of Man, pp. 124-25. Teilhard's Activation now appears as Activation of Energy (New York: Harcourt Brace Jovanovich, Inc., 1971).

8. Teilhard, "Esquisse dialectique," p. 155 as cited by Mooney, Making of Man, p. 129; also see Phenomenon of Man, p. 308, n. 2; also p. 294.

9. Teilhard, Phenomenon of Man, pp. 53-66; Faricy, Teilhard's Theology, pp. 29-30, 33-46.

10. Teilhard, Future of Man, p. 97.

11. Pierre Teilhard de Chardin, Human Energy, trans. J.M. Cohen (New York: Harcourt Brace Jovanovich, Inc., 1971) pp. 53-92.

12. Teilhard, Christianity and Evolution, p. 135.

13. Ibid., p. 155.

14. Ibid., pp. 182-83.

15. Teilhard, "Comment je vois," p. 17 and n. 26. I am using a translation from Christopher F. Mooney, S.J., Teilhard de Chardin and the Mystery of Christ (New York: Harper & Row, 1966), p. 175.

16. Pierre Teilhard de Chardin, The Divine Milieu (New York: Harper Torchbooks, 1965), pp. 123-26.

17. Teilhard, Phenomenon of Man, p. 310.

18. See Mooney, The Mystery of Christ, pp. 169-70, where he cites several of Teilhard's works.

19. Faricy, Teilhard's Theology, p. 142, where he quotes Teilhard, "Du Cosmos à la Cosmogénèse," Oeuvres de P. Teilhard de Chardin, v. 7 (Paris: Seuil, 1955-65), p. 268.

20. Teilhard, "Mon Univers," Oeuvres, v. 9, p. 109, n. 2, as cited by Mooney, Mystery of Christ, p. 126. This essay now appears in Pierre Teilhard de Chardin, Science and Christ, trans. René Hague (New York: Harper & Row, 1969), pp. 37-85. Teilhard speaks often of love as the sole energy which can further true human progress. See his Phenomenon of Man, pp. 264-68; Human Energy, pp. 145-55.

21. Teilhard, Phenomenon of Man, p. 313.

22. Teilhard, Christianity and Evolution, pp. 36-8.

23. Ibid., p. 54; see also pp. 40, 149, 190-91.

24. Ibid., pp. 39, 41, 51; see also Faricy, Teilhard's Theology, pp. 158-59. For a brief indication of more recent trends in Catholic theology which are compatible with Teilhard's basic theology of Original Sin see Faricy, Ibid., p. 161, n. 51. See also Piet Schoonenberg, S.J., Man and Sin, trans. Joseph Donceel, S.J. (Chicago: Henry Regnery, 1965).

25. Ibid., pp. 135-41.

26. Ibid., pp. 46-7, 52.

27. Ibid., p. 193.

28. Ibid., pp. 194-96, 150.

29. Ibid., pp. 196-97.

30. Ibid., p. 53.

31. Ibid., p. 80; see also pp. 21-4, 149, 84.

32. Ibid., pp. 84-5.

33. Ibid., p. 85. Emphasis is editor's not Teilhard's.

34. Ibid., pp. 163, 217.

35. Pierre Teilhard de Chardin, "Essai d'integration de l'homme dans l'univers," as quoted by Mooney, Mystery of Christ, p. 119.

36. Mooney, Mystery of Christ, p. 133. Also see Faricy, Teilhard's Theology, pp. 163-68. In a note on p. 167 Faricy takes issue—rightly so, I think—with Mooney's view (Mystery of Christ, p. 133) that, in effect, only the creative, unitive, or positive aspect of Christ's redemptive activity seems operative in Teilhard's theory. Mooney criticizes Teilhard for not strongly affirming the reparative work of Christ and for not linking it with the idea of overcoming man's refusal to love.

37. Faricy, Teilhard's Theology, pp. 173-74, 176.

38. Teilhard, Human Energy, pp. 105-06.

39. Ibid., p. 29.

40. For Teilhard's development of these three principles see Human Energy, pp. 106-09; also see Faricy, Teilhard's Theology, p. 180.

41. Teilhard, Phenomenon of Man, pp. 221, 224, 232-233; also see Teilhard, Future of Man, p. 291; Mooney, Making of Man, p. 122.

42. Pierre Teilhard de Chardin, The Vision of the Past, trans. J.M. Cohen (New York: Harper & Row, 1966), pp. 212-13; also see Pierre Teilhard de Chardin, Building the Earth, trans. Noël Lindsay (Wilkes Barre: Dimension Books, 1965), p. 54.

43. Teilhard, Phenomenon of Man, pp. 282-83.

44. Teilhard, Future of Man, pp. 201, 57; also see Teilhard, Phenomenon of Man, p. 263.

45. Teilhard, Future of Man, p. 202.

46. Ibid., p. 203. Throughout the presentation of the three principles all quotations are taken from this passage.

47. Donald P. Gray, "Teilhard's Vision of Love," Dimensions of the Future: The Spirituality of Teilhard de Chardin, eds. Marvin Kessler, S.J. and Bernard Brown, S.J. (Washington: Corpus Books, 1968), pp. 73-98 at 74. See also Teilhard, Phenomenon of Man, pp. 265, 267; the idea that all true union differentiates is a recurrent one in Teilhard's writings; see Science and Christ, p. 137; Future of Man, pp. 55-59.

48. Teilhard, Science and Christ, pp. 167-71.

49. Teilhard, Future of Man, p. 98. Also see Henri de Lubac, S.J., Teilhard de Chardin: The Man and His Meaning, trans. René Hague (New York: Hawthorne Books, 1965), p. 37, n. 28.

50. Teilhard, Human Energy, pp. 85-91.

51. Teilhard, Science and Christ, p. 34. In this section I am indebted also to Faricy, Teilhard's Theology, pp. 181-84, 196-202.

52. Teilhard, "Réflexions sur le bonheur," Cahiers Pierre Teilhard de Chardin, II (Paris, 1960), p. 61, as cited by Mooney, Making of Man, p. 139.

53. Teilhard, Science and Christ, pp. 66-71.

54. References here and in the preceding paragraph are to Ibid., pp. 72-73.

55. Teilhard, Vision of the Past, p. 214; Building the Earth, p. 111; Future of Man, p. 78; Phenomenon of Man, pp. 268-72.

56. Mooney, Making of Man, pp. 130-148.

57. Teilhard, "Turmoil or Genesis?," (1947), Future of Man, pp. 222-235; Mooney makes reference to Teilhard's theory of "preliminary sketch" (ébauche) in Making of Man, pp. 62-3 and p. 171, n. 35. A similar view of man's contribution to the appearance of God's future is held by Wolfhart Pannenberg, Theology and the Kingdom of God (Phila.: Westminister Press, 1969), p. 126.

58. As examples of the view which describes Teilhard's morality in terms exclusively of the love energy see Fernand Arsenault, "L'Ethique sociale chez Teilhard de Chardin," Sciences Religieuses/Studies in Religion, 1, No. 1 (1971), 25-44, and Pierre Burney, "Sketch for a Morality of Love: A Tentative Application of Teilhardian Methods," The Teilhard Review, 4 (Winter, 1969-70), 60-71. Other studies of Teilhard's morality are Andre Devaux, "Teilhard et la construction d'une morale pour notre temps," Revue Teilhard de Chardin, 6, No. 23 (1965), 31-8, and Denis Mermod, La Morale de Teilhard (Paris, 1967), the latter of which I have been unable to consult.

59. Teilhard, Divine Milieu, pp. 151-52.

60. Ibid., pp. 152-54.

61. Ibid., pp. 154-55.

62. Teilhard, Phenomenon of Man, p. 232, n. 1.

63. Teilhard, Future of Man, pp. 75-7.

64. Teilhard, Science and Christ, pp. 67-8.

65. Teilhard, Divine Milieu, p. 63; see also Henri de Lubac, S.J., The Religion of Teilhard de Chardin, trans. René Hague (New York: Doubleday Image Books, 1968), pp. 301-09.

66. See Teilhard's Personalized Universe," in Robert O. Johann, Building the Human (New York: Herder & Herder, 1968), pp. 96-113 at 113.

AWAITING THE FUTURE OF GOD IN ACTIVE HOPE: MOLTMANN'S POLITICAL ETHICS FOR AN "EXISTENCE IN EXODUS"

Introduction

Since our intent in this study is simply to open up a greater place for the virtue of hope in the task of ethical reflection and to indicate further how the reality of hope actually functions in this task, this chapter on Jürgen Moltmann's theology will focus on those aspects of his thought which highlight most clearly his attempt to restore some hope in an ultimate synthesis between the action of God's love in history and the labors undertaken by human beings in obedience to God.

We shall see first how Moltmann's understanding of revelation as promise makes a "God of hope" the most appropriate title for the divine being. From a promise made by God and from the history that this promise opens up for us, the Judeo-Christian tradition derives its political nature, and calls us to an attitude of hope lived out in a critical transformation of society through a process of negating the negatives of present existence. Under the shadow of the cross as it is illuminated by the resurrection of Christ, we must translate our hope for the future promised by God into a life of obedient and suffering love, which remains always anxious to transcend both the pains and the comforts of the status quo through an identification with the wounded of the earth. God's promise regarding our future is two-dimensional. It contains not only the good news which radically alters our human expectations, but also it presents us with the challenge of God's expectations for us. Liberated, then, by the gospel of God's promise, and directed by the challenge it raises, our hope is kept alive and active in the ethical struggle to anticipate the new future of God by living in correspondence with that future even now. To conclude this chapter we will see where Moltmann's thinking puts him in relation to Teilhard.

The Political Nature of Christianity

Without denying the other formative elements in Moltmann's thinking, it is safe to say that the Marxist critique of religion serves as the background against which he prefers to formulate much of his understanding of the messianic faith of Christianity. Integral to the Christian faith, says Moltmann, is an element of protest which is so vital, that our groping for freedom in faith simultaneously exposes us to the categorical imperative to struggle for the liberation of suffering creation from afflictions. Failure to meet the real demand for the world's liberation results in the gospel being used to justify the oppressive and panic-filled condition of the world as it is. What is needed today is not so much a reinterpretation of heaven through a process of deymthologization, but rather a critical reshaping of earth, politics, and law. The radical consequence of such reordering will be a revolutionary advancement toward the realization of human freedom.

For Moltmann, the reason for the critical involvement of Christians in the world is always the cross of Christ seen as an expression of real human affliction. In the shadow of the cross, the resurrection takes on the significance of a true protest against human affliction. Thus the proclamation of the cross of the resurrected Christ, far from being an opiate which intoxicates and incapacitates people, is rather "the ferment of new freedom," calling and leading people to draw on the power of the resurrection in resisting the conditions of oppression which bind humanity in body or spirit. Moltmann insists that the gospel proclamation must be concerned with how the biblical announcement of freedom can be mediated to the oppressions of the present and even directed toward the deliverance of humanity from present misery by means of political action. The requirements for every theological hermeneutic are that it become the theoretical basis for practice and that it serve as "the entrance to future truth." Only in this way is theology likely to enhance the future freedom of human beings.[1]

With this general understanding of religion, Moltmann looks at what he calls the modern schism from which many Christians and atheists are suffering today. To the extent that Christians believe in a "God without future," Moltmann suggests that people who will the future of the earth have no choice but to join company with atheism and seek a "future without God." But in this dichotomy, the scars of battle are worn as clearly by those who hold fast to a God without future in a faith without hope, as by those who seek a future without God in a hope without faith. Moltmann, however, like Teilhard, realizes that we do not have to ride forever the horns of this dilemma.

86

The knots of history, which have bound Christianity with the past and unbelievers with the future, can be loosened, "but only if Christians call again upon the 'God of hope' of the Old and New Testaments and testify to him practically and concretely in responsibility for the present."[2] To understand why Moltmann speaks of a "God of hope," it is necessary to realize that for him divine revelation enters human history precisely as "promise," and in so doing radically changes the nature and shape of human expectation.

Revelation as Promise by the "God of Hope"

The observation has been made by some that the "theology of hope" is somewhat of a misnomer, and that a more accurate description of this particular theological endeavor would speak rather of a theology of promise.[3] There is a good reason for this observation, because Moltmann spearheads a theological movement which is grounded ineluctably in Yahweh's word of promise which became flesh in Jesus Christ. On the basis of Old Testament theology, Moltmann believes that revelation is most accurately perceived not as an answer to a question nor as a disclosure of something veiled or hidden, but rather as God's promise, wherein "God reveals himself in the form of promise and in the history that is marked by promise." Because the word which reveals God basically embodies the character of promise, it is a hope-giving word and is therefore eschatological.[4]

In the New Testament and the revelation-event of Christ's death and resurrection, Moltmann finds a modification of the implications of God's promise; what appears here is a new reality, a new and other future, a **novum ultimum**, which consists in a universal eschatological future for humanity, far transcending those Israelo-centric expectations wherein the future is pictured as "the occupation of a new land, as the setting up of a new David and a new Zion, as a new exodus, as a new covenant." The concept behind all these Old Testament images is that of a " 'renewal' and return of what is past and lost, so that beginning and end correspond to each other."[5] In the death and resurrection of Christ, however, the believer's expectation becomes a hope against hope which conquers death itself. And without this final victory, which Moltmann, like Teilhard, sees as critically important for the human spirit, our commitment to social and political activity is internally jeopardized.

The underlying character of promise is that of "a declaration which announces the coming of a reality that does not yet exist." Consequently, the effect of living in a history which is shaped by promise is to situate human beings in an atmosphere of unrest with regard to themselves and their present world, with the result that they are directed toward the future in a process of "leaving things behind and striking out toward new horizons as yet unseen." In light of the incongruity between what is promised and what is presently experienced, a situation arises in which people tend either to measure the word of promise by the standard of given reality, or to measure present reality by the standard of the word of promise. In the first instance doubt prevails, while in the second, hope succeeds. But always the decision to hope is justified only because the promise is situated ultimately in the faithfulness of God; it is his fidelity which makes for continuity throughout the historical process. And yet, because the promise is the word of a God who remains not only always faithful but also living, it is only to be expected that there may be reformation, development, and interpretation in the history of that promise. Indeed, given "the inexhaustibility of the God of promise, who never exhausts himself in any historic reality but comes 'to rest' only in a reality that wholly corresponds to him," it follows that every present fulfillment of the eschatological promise becomes at once the basis and liberation of a still greater hope.[6]

For Moltmann, the word of promise breaks into events and divides reality into two parts: one "which is passing and can be left behind, and another which must be expected and sought." In this way an opening is made for the development of a real history which must be understood as being a result of the promise, and not as a teleological process, for "it is not evolution, progress and advance that separate time into yesterday and tomorrow," but only the word of promise. Thus, there is no doubt but that Israel was able to experience her life as truly open history only by virtue of the fact "that God was revealed . . . in his promises." In a real sense Israel's future was given to her, and it is only because he is faithful to his promises, that the God of Israel becomes a God of hope among his people for all times.[7]

In Moltmann's thinking, the "wandering people of God" and the "God of hope" are closely joined, for God's people do not act without purpose and direction. They are a forward-moving people who live with a promise in their ears and hope in their hearts for a new future; it is only because of their eschatologically-oriented faith that they can sustain the effort to change the world rather than simply to interpret it, and to transform existence rather than merely to elucidate it. In a remarkable way the eschatological dimension of faith receives an unexpected support in the broken covenant and in the subsequent experience of guilt on the part of the Jewish people, because once the guarantees contained in the traditions of election were challenged by Israel's guilt, there was only one thing upon which Israel could rely, namely, "Yahweh's new act in history, prophetically proclaimed." Thus, for Israel the basis of salvation shifts from the past to the future, and her faith changes from a living memory into a living hope, so that throughout her catastrophes, and in spite of the discontinuities of history, she finds her own continuity "in the transcending faithfulness of God." Her prophets have rightfully instilled in her the expectation of new acts on the part of God as he embodies his covenantal relationship with his people in history.[8]

Israel's concern, however, with the prophecies of the new age has the strange effect of vitalizing the memory of her past history, because the facts of the past are real anticipations of the new future. The past is the locus and context of the promise, in which the "good news" of salvation is not only announced but also offered. Thus the people of God live neither in a remote past nor in a distant future, for both the memory of the past promises and the anticipation of the promises' fulfillment in a new future come together in our present hopefulness in the fidelity of God.[9]

When Moltmann describes the faith-stance of God's people as eschatological, it is evident that he understands eschatology in a quite definite way as "the **doctrine of hope**," which is concerned as such both with the future that human beings can hope for and with the course of action that must be undertaken in order to bring "the hoped-for future into the sufferings of the present age." Against the universal horizon of eschatology the reality of the world as history is revealed; faith in Christ is seen as practical hope for the coming of God, and both the past and the present are respected as the history of the future of God; finally, the present is understood as the "presence of the future." In this context, theology as eschatology comes to speak not of a "God above us," nor of a "God within us," but rather of "God ahead of us, in front of us," "the God of hope," and "God of the Exodus."[10]

89

It is also against the universal horizon of eschatology that the essentially political structure of theology appears, since God's people, standing in the dawn of a new future, invariably face the challenge of bringing "the 'power of the future world' into the trouble spots of the present, personally, socially, and politically." Thus, life within the history of the promise has an immediate effect upon the meaning of Christianity's mission. We shall return later to Moltmann's political hermeneutic, but for now it must suffice simply to say that Christianity, in light of the promised future, has found a new companionship with the world and its social and political institutions. For now, if both the church and the world stand together before that future which traditionally has been called the Judgment and the Kingdom of God, it follows that the differences between them can be seen only as relative. In Moltmann's terms, "the lines of separation no longer go spatially through body and soul, spirituality and secularity, faith and politics, church and world, but are found temporally in all areas of life between the power of the past and the 'power of the future world'."[11] Allegiance to God implies, for Moltmann, the decision to be guided by the power of the future, which, for Teilhard, as we saw in the previous chapter, is the power of love.

Negating the Negatives of the Present: Hoping and Planning for the Future

In view of the conflict between the power of the past and the power of the future world, Moltmann describes history in various ways: it is the experimental field of the future, the difference between exodus and arrival, or between experience and hope. One thing is certain, however: the future "always rebounds from its own realization in history and becomes again a not yet realized future of the whole of being." In the discussion of man's present relationship to the future and his anticipations regarding it, Moltmann makes the important observations that human expectations of the future must be realistic, and that the in-rushing of the future cannot be passively awaited. He notes that our expectations of the future are motivated not by visions and by dreams alone, but also by pain and suffering, and that in these latter we are nearer to reality than in dreams and visions. Thus in the midst of suffering it is easier to say that thus and so shall not be in the future, than to say that one thing or another shall be. In other words, what full freedom and humanity

90

are is hard to say, since no one has yet experienced the kingdom of freedom; however, we know too well what inhumanity and its effects are. For this reason, then, we must relate to both the present and the future in a process of negating the present negatives, and this is an undertaking which has the advantage of providing a dynamic thrust for the movement through history without the stereotyped imposition of historical definitions of freedom and happiness. As Moltmann puts it: "Hope in the positive is alive in suffering from the negative. Hope in the happiness of the future is realistically present and effective in the criticism of present misery."[12]

While he recognizes that we have no full positive knowledge of the kingdom of freedom or of the qualitatively new future initiated by God for us and our world, Moltmann, nevertheless, insists upon that future's present influence within the historical process. The kingdom of freedom is, in fact, closely linked with the present process of negating history's negatives, for where God proclaims his presence the God-forsakenness of the world is experienced as suffering. But more than this, hearing the promise for the future of the world leads to the discovery also of hope for the world; with hope in one's heart, one begins to love the world and to suffer from its present conditions. Moreover, when people begin to suffer from unfreedom and no longer submit to slavery as to their destiny, they enjoy the first experience of freedom. It is in this way that Christianity and her message cease to be "honey" and become "salt," because now the kingdom of freedom, the new future, even though present in promise and anticipation only, appears as a crucial motivating element in the continuing struggle to overcome the miseries and afflictions of mankind.[13] In other words, to the extent that the word of God's coming kingdom of freedom stands as a contradiction to the economic, political and racial alienation being endured today, it follows that "the all-embracing vision of God must be linked with the economic liberation of man from hunger, with the political freeing of man from oppression by other men, and with the human emancipation of man from racial humiliation."[14]

In effect, what Moltmann argues for is recognition of the fact that an individual's personal meaning is contingent upon his or her involvement in the struggle for the humanization of society and the world. There is no doubt but that on this point Moltmann's political hermeneutics shares the Marxist concern to co-ordinate theory and practice or to translate religious myths into action. From this perspective, hermeneutics is not a question simply of demythologization in the sense of a movement from one set of symbols to another; rather, the only adequate interpretation of the gospel is its inauguration within the realm of human existence of the liberation which takes its life from Jesus Christ. The gospel message, correctly understood, must inspire us to the "revolutionary realization of freedom within present conditions."[15]

It is wrong to conclude, therefore, that Moltmann expects the spirit of opposition which is stirred up by the gospel to exhaust itself in a negating process which is simply reactionary. He intends, rather, the instigation also of a critical and constructive dialectic with the present historical situation. The intimations of a new future are judged meaningless and useless if they do not result in immediate commitment to the search for justice and the struggle for human freedom. The hope which is inspired by the gospel is meant to serve as a catalyst for imaginative planning, for in light of the gospel, Christian hope comes to reflect on the data of real possibilities which are simply unavailable to, or overlooked by, an unimaginative political "realism." Thus, for Moltmann, "the new" is always preceded by a promise, a dream, an anticipation, and thus is never "wholly new;" at the same time, he is most insistent that the future is not accessible by a mere extrapolation from presently-perceived possibilities. Rather, in the gospel's light there exists an interplay between faith-rooted hope (expectation) and rational planning (initiation), such that they constitute distinct but somewhat inseparable means of relating to the future.[16]

In specific situations of human oppression, then, such biblical images as the Exodus, the prophetic ministry of Christ, and the central symbols of death and resurrection, reveal possibilities for acting which are in keeping with God's promises. This means simply that these biblical symbols offer a new horizon against which to form social and political programs; in no way, however, is factual knowledge or discriminating judgment rendered otiose, for it is not at all the intention of a political hermeneutics of the gospel to limit the scope of moral deliberation, but rather to broaden it.[17]

For this reason, Walter Capps suggests that the hermeneutical enterprise shifts from demythologizing to "pro-mythologizing," by which he means that Christianity's task now is to find the image and story which are so provocative, creative and effective as to initiate action to shape the future of humanity.[18] It is for this same reason, moreover, that Moltmann believes that through the messianic vision of Christianity, religion becomes a kind of "proligion" in which faith in God is joined with "hope in the liberation of man on a new earth and under a new heaven."[19] Thus, spurred on by the discrepancy between the present and the promised future, Christians must live in history with an attitude of critical and creative hope which both allows and compels them to negate the injustices of the present and to propose positive alternatives to their perpetuation.

For Moltmann, the hope of Christians bears witness to their realization of the present's potential which exists by reason of the abiding covenant of a faithful God. This covenant affects believers in two ways: it introduces the good news under whose inspiration we are encouraged to move toward the freedom of the future; at the same time, it establishes certain commands under whose direction we must carry out the exploration of our promised future. Both the good news and the commands are assimilated into our lives and thus affect the nature of our involvement in the process of history. But the promised future not only makes us more directly and immediately aware of the things that need changing; it also highlights the potential of the present against the background of the gift of God's future. By means of his promise, the power of God in the future becomes active here and now both by illuminating the present's potential for change and by consequently inspiring us to hope and to put our hope to work.

The effect of the word of promise is not only to give hope where there is none, but also to remind us that some of history's potential will remain unfulfilled despite our efforts, and that thus our hope will remain unsatisfied in time and space. In this way Christian hope serves as a constant threat and challenge to any political humanism's tendency to transform its own periodic successes over prevailing injustices into ideological pogroms. Thus, in its formative influence upon the shape of human existence by providing a transcendent criterion to which we must look as we critique the inequities of the present, the word of God's promise affords us the only guarantee of continued flexibility and liberation in the struggle to discover and maintain the full dimensions of humanity. Indeed, only in this way can we resist the temptation to replace one form of inhumanity with another.

Theology of the Cross: A Call to Obedient Love

Our discussion of Moltmann's theology must now turn its attention to the role which Christ and the events of his life and death play in establishing and maintaining the dynamics of Christian hope. We might reasonably expect that the resurrection of Christ must figure predominantly in any exposition of the vitality of hope in Christian life, and such is indeed the case. And yet, as Moltmann is quick to point out, the followers of Christ, unlike Christ himself, are not yet beyond the reach of death, so that the only way in which resurrection is present to them is "in hope and as promise." Moreover, the life of hope must be sustained for the present time under the shadow of the cross which stands as a symbol of the eschatological presence of the resurrection in the midst of the trials of history. This means, of course, that the only way in which the life of the resurrection is here granted to Christians is in the form of the theology of the cross of Christ.

Insofar as the new future is only eschatologically present, believers do not enjoy a full sharing in the lordship of Christ but, nevertheless, they are still "led by hope into the tensions and antitheses of obedience and suffering in the world." The call to obedience reaches believers "in the body and on earth" and through their obedience both the "earth and the body are set within the horizon of the expectation of the coming lordship of Christ." In hopeful obedience Christians take on the "sufferings of discipleship" of Christ, and their identification with Christ impels them in turn to assume the sufferings of the world so as to move the world to the glory that is promised it.[20]

The realization of this promised glory demands, of course, the "infinite creativity" of God and is, in fact, a new **creatio ex nihilo.** As such, the only assurance given us of this fulfillment is its "sign" and "anticipation" in the "raising of Christ from the dead." But the event of Christ's resurrection is not historically verifiable as yet, since of its very nature it is subject only to "eschatological verification." And yet the resurrection does provide us with a sort of "negative theology" of the Christian life, for it signifies the approach and entrance of what is "qualitatively new" into the total personal history of Christ, especially as that history was marked by the form of the cross. This is to say, that in his resurrection, Christ "has been received into the future of the 'kingdom of God' and the coming glory of God." And yet, because historical images and categories cannot be attached to the resurrection by way of explaining and verifying it, the road is thus cleared for the coming of God by means of a removal of all "representations of the fantasies of hope."[21]

Moltmann insists that Christ's cross and resurrection belong inseparably together and interpret each other, and that Christian hope is founded in the total person and entire history of Christ, and not on the isolated event of his resurrection. In no way is Christ's resurrection to be seen solely as "an arrow pointing to the hitherto unknown future of God and man." Rather, this future has now taken on flesh in the crucified Christ and thus has become involved in the present. The cross of the risen Christ has come to mean that "resurrection, life, and freedom" are "mediated through Jesus to those who live in darkness and in the midst of death." Moltmann continues:

> Jesus' resurrection may have been understood as a **sign** of hope for a God-forsaken mankind. But only his cross was the real mediation of this hope for the hopeless. Thus the cross is the present form of the resurrection. The coming glory of God is mirrored in the face of the crucified one. We are therefore able to say that Jesus' resurrection is only **indirectly**, but the meaning of his cross is **directly**, the foundation of the Christian hope for justice and life.[22]

The memory of Christ's cross serves to protect Christian hope from naive optimism and its inevitable disillusionment. Because our hope is born of the cross, it is truly a crucified hope, a "hope against hope." While the resurrection enables us to hope for a life where love flourishes without reservation, it is also true that in the spirit of the cross, our "creative and self-giving love mirrors future resurrection under the conditions of the present life." To the extent, then, that our hope is embodied in an obedient love whereby we make the cause of the vulnerable of the earth our own, we truly anticipate our resurrection into full life and freedom "in the reverse movement of the incarnation, of self-oblation and faithful labor." In other words, love, which is freely given and freely suffered, creates new life out of nothing, and thus becomes the resurrection in this life's time and place.[23]

Because the cross is the real mediation of hope for the hopeless, the theology of the cross is made the basis of Moltmann's political theology and serves as the concrete expression of his theology of liberation. The term "political theology" designates the milieu in which Christian theology must be articulated today. In a real sense, then, political theology is a hermeneutical tool or category by means of which an attempt is made "to interpret the dangerous memory of the messianic message of Christ within the conditions of contemporary society" so that we might free people in a practical way from the oppressions of this society and thus help in preparing the way for the eschatological freedom promised them by God. For Moltmann, the eyes of Christian hope are not focused simply on the open future, but on "the future of the hopeless." Thus, the cry of Luther that "the cross alone is our theology" resounds in Moltmann's contention "that the dangerous memory of the cross is our political iconoclasm; the cross is our hope for the politics of liberation. The liberating memory of the crucified Jesus compels Christians to a critical political theology."[24]

Hope in the future of God and in the ultimate liberation of human beings does not allow Christians to await this future passively. Rather, they must seek and strive for the new future and, in fact, begin to live in correspondence to it even now through the active renewal of life and its conditions of possibility; they must struggle, in short, to realize the new future here and now to the greatest extent possible. Out of its passion for what has been made possible by God in Christ, Christian hope also derives a "passion for what is possible" through the efforts of human beings. And yet, because it has been gifted with the "better promises" (Heb. 8:6) of a **novum ultimum,** "a new creation of all things by the God of the resurrection of Jesus Christ," Christian hope always qualifies the presumptuous expectations of any utopian hopes "of better human freedom, of successful life, of justice and dignity for our fellow men, of control of the possibilities of nature . . ." Knowing that nothing can be "very good" until "all things are become new," believing hope views futuristic movements of historic change as precursory and, thus, provisional movements whose goals are penultimate and hence flexible.[25] Christian expectation is always focused ultimately on Jesus Christ who alone offers radical newness. Provisory as the futuristic movements of the world may be, however, they necessarily confront Christians with the challenge of participation. One particularly provocative question that believers must face arises in relation to their involvement in such futuristic movements when they take the form of revolution.

Revolution and Transcendence

In his irreligious critique of religion Marx had effectively confronted theology with the categorical imperative "to overthrow all circumstances in which man is a humiliated, an enslaved, a forsaken and a despised being." Moltmann, in principle, accepts the Marxist challenge, and thus describes the goal of Christian social action as the creation of a situation in which every person "may become a more abundant, upright, sovereign, and purposeful" individual. Concretely, this means that not only must Christians be involved in programs for the alleviation of hunger, poverty, and illness, but also that they must give fruitful recognition to every individual's need for human acknowledgment and appreciation. Moreover, even in the midst of a rising prosperity, it becomes ever more apparent that people may suffer not only from hunger and disease, or from lack of recognition, but also from something less tangible—a sense of nothingness, frustration, and ennui. People can gain victories over hunger and poverty only to find a stronger enemy, a life of boredom. In this new battle, Moltmann suggests that Christianity, without explaining away the experience of boredom and frustration, can, nevertheless, provide men with a sense of purpose and direction.[26]

In this context the purpose of Christianity and the church is described by Moltmann in various ways; the church is here "for the Kingdom of God and the freedom of the children of God, and in this sense it is here for the world." Or, it may be said that Christianity exists for the coming of our true humanity and for the humanizing of the social order, in which case the church cannot be satisfied simply with nurturing a liberated, but isolated, personal existence, nor with the creation of underground forms of intimate fellowship; her impact must rather be felt throughout the social milieu.[27] For this reason, Christianity's hope in a new future and a new creation does not change the fact that the new criterion of theology and of faith is found in praxis:

> Christian hope dare not evacuate the present by dreaming about the future; nor may it compensate for any empty present by dreaming about the future. It must, rather, draw the hoped-for future already into the misery of the present and use it in practical initiatives for overcoming this misery. Through criticism and protest, on the one hand, and creative

imagination and action, on the other, we can avail ourselves of freedom for the future.[28]

Of its essence, then, Christian hope is "a source of creative and inventive imagination in the service of love." As such, while it may indeed affirm that it is God who "gives comfort and promises righteousness to the guilty, life to the dying, freedom to the oppressed, and true humanity to the dehumanized," believing hope is also constantly "alert for what is correspondingly possible in the present."[29] Still, there is never any question but that the crucial point for Moltmann and Christians is that the coming realm of total freedom is always more than the fragments of any free life which we may achieve in history; this view, however, does not demand a debilitating division between heaven and earth:

> If we conceive that salvation be the transcendence for the immanent emancipation movement of men, then the Christians' "beyond" is not a compensation or "the opium of the people" any more, but is the power and the ferment of emancipation here and now. Traditionally we have always combined reconciliation with God with the conservation of the earth. But there is no reconciliation without transformation, that is, without personal repentance and social revolution.[30]

Moltmann is deeply convinced that faith in the God who makes all things new can serve to strengthen the movements of social transformation; at the same time, this faith can laugh at those who fashion themselves demigods. In other words, "freedom for revolutionary action can be bound up in faith with freedom from the coercion of revolutionary action." Faith in God affords a way out of the legalism, the moralism, and the ideology of revolutions; thus the possibility is opened up for revolutionaries who are at once serious, self-critical, and joyous—freed from the works of the law. These people can laugh about their involvement "because they are the forerunners of a yet greater revolution, in which God will abolish even greater oppositions than any human revolution can envision."[31]

For Moltmann, there is no way in which a true Christian revolution can be arbitrary or self-seeking. It must be initiated only with the intention of preparing a future in which people may enjoy

"freedom and possibility and the opportunity for something new."
We must recall, however, that Christians profess that what is radically
new is a function of God's authority and power. For this reason, an
authentic Christian revolution is always modulated by the remembrance that its intervention in history is an attempt to change a
world that is on the way to the **eschaton** when God will finally
present the newness he enjoys giving.[32]

The present struggle of Christians comes to life under the light of
the hoped-for future whose reality is translated into the power of the
present in such a way that the energy of hope is a creative participation in the life of that future. Thus, Christian hope is revolutionary,
but not in any traditional sense of involving reactionary restoration
or renovation. Rather, its power is "turned forward" and tries "to
direct the course of human history" toward the new future. Revolution is really "provolution," and Christian hope espouses only those
revolutionary movements which are forerunners of the "yet greater
revolution" expressed in the "Behold, I make all things new" (Rev.
21:5) of the new creation.[33] And so, unlike the Marxist who confines hope to the sphere of "that-which-is-not-yet" and thus links
hope for a new future only with what people can still accomplish,
Moltmann emphasizes that for Christians there is hope also in the
sphere of "that-which-is-no-longer"; in this way hope is connected
also with what people must bear in suffering, in pain, and in dying.
Christians hope not only when they are young but also when they
are old and incapacitated, when they can no longer help themselves
and even when death robs them of all hope.[34]

Moltmann's conviction that the Christian is one whose hope must
be active in love, comes into clearest focus in his discussion of revolutionary violence. His position is expressed succinctly in the thesis:
"The problem of violence and nonviolence is an illusory problem.
There is only the question of the justified and unjustified use of
force and the question of whether the means are proportionate to
the ends." This thesis is actually somewhat misleading, however, for
in his exposition of it, and in subsequent reflections, Moltmann is
not nearly so callously satisfied with the use of violence as this thesis
might suggest. While not ruling out the use of violence on principle,
he does argue that if disproportionate means are employed, the
humane goals of the revolution are betrayed. Inhumanity in the
midst of the revolutionary struggle will never produce the revolutionary goal of a more fully realized humanity; thus, if revolutionaries

enter into "the diabolical circle of violence and counterviolence," they must do so with great restraint. Moltmann feels strongly that the means of resistance used by Christians "must be different and better than those of the opposition if they are to bewilder the opposition." Speaking figuratively, the ploy must be to force the atomic powers into guerrilla warfare, and "the poker players of power" into "the chess game of reason."[35]

Not everything, then, receives approval within the framework of Christian revolutionary hope. But if sensitive Christians under the impulse of love should come to find the sufferings of others intolerable, their final recourse may be to revolutionary violence. In this case, it is a question of their desire for personal innocence having to yield to social responsibility. In other words, in extreme circumstances as might be verified in life under the rule of an established tyrant, Christian responsibility "demands a love that is ready to incur guilt in order to save." Even as the last resort of Christians, however, violence is not graced with the title of being justified. It remains as a possible but alien duty of love; as such, it necessarily entails a guilt for which Christians must seek forgiveness. For Moltmann, then, there are some occasions when violence "can be answered for," even if it cannot be approved. His reason for this position is that he sees "the responsible action of love" rather than the "idealistic principle of nonviolence" as consonant with the gospel.

In addition to suggesting that Christians can give an account of the violence that they engage in out of a love "which desires to put an end to evil," Moltmann offers two other propositions. First, he suggests that in tyrannical situations, there is no justification for non-violence in the sense of nonresistance, for such an attitude only serves to encourage violence, and thus inactive Christians would face the possibility of incurring a "more irredeemable guilt." Moltmann's second proposition warns that in response to tyrannical situations, "action and failure to act are not the same . . . in the sense that either way one incurs guilt," for in fact the "more irredeemable guilt" in most cases surrounds sins of omission.[36] Thus, although Moltmann allows Christians the possibility of engaging in violent action, he never sees them as going into violence easily, quickly or happily.

In the presence of the coming new future of God, the task of Christians is to maintain a precious and precarious balance. Since human nature is grounded and developed within a history whose process and meaning are adequately grasped only from the perspective of eschatology, Christians, living in the dawn of hope (Rom. 13:11-14), are called to cut a path "between optimistic chiliasm and apocalyptic lethargy." Thus while "good works do not build the kingdom of God," hope in this coming kingdom must, nevertheless, assume ethical forms within history, for with their eschatological vision the people of God are expected to be a source of unrest within every historical society.[37]

For Moltmann, Christian consciousness is always, above all, a "consciousness of mission." Under the "power of the resurrection" the spirit of Christian hope accepts and endures the "cross of the present," but its sole concern never ceases to be the reconciliation of all things with their real future. In light of its fundamental "missionary" character, Christian hope can remain alive only through patience, which "alone is able to survive the tension of the hope of history." Through its art of patience, Christian hope can take upon itself the torture and the pain of the negatives that the still-unredeemed present is heir to; it does so, however, without either resignation or illusions.[38] Christian hope, finally, is an attitude of patient unrest, and Christians are those who are free neither to do nothing nor to do everything.

Thus when Christians bring their vision and their hope to bear on the issue of revolutionary involvement, it can only be expected that their active participation in revolutions will be less than fanatical, because they are commissioned more to anticipate the new future than to realize or create it. The situation is such because if revolutionary activity against the world's injustice is the political implication of the resurrection, so also the political implication of Christ's crucifixion must be the principle of non-violent resistance.[39] Surely Christians are freed to forge a pathway into God's future. Deprived of the security of old and present structures of existence, they may dare an exploration into God and into his intentions for a new creation. But believers are also relieved of the burden of playing God. Realizing that they are not God, Christians may make the most of their humanity without pretending either that all things can be done by them or that they ought to be. By allowing God to be God, and by accepting their own humanity, Christians enjoy the liberty to play, along with the responsibility to work. Their world-transforming love is guided finally by their world-surpassing hope by means of which they escape the convulsions of anxiety and vengeance.[40]

While the atmosphere created by the Christian dispensation is one which needs the creative contributions of human beings for its preservation and extension, it also affords believers an opportunity to breathe freely in the conviction that after all it is the Lord who says, "Behold, I make all things new." And so, in light of the primacy of God and his abiding fidelity to his liberating word of promise, the new future is neither totally unknown nor totally open. Its shape is outlined in the covenantal relationship, and thus the history of Christian spiritual and ethical endeavor knows where to look for guidance in directing its efforts into the future. In order to understand the basis and dynamism of Moltmann's ethical reflections, it is necessary to consider further the covenantal promises of God which serve as the key to Moltmann's theology in that they alone reveal the "God of hope."

The Promises as Gospel and Command, and the Role of Christian Obedience

Thus far our analysis has shown that Moltmann's theology takes the following course. Through God's revelation of his covenantal promises, believers receive an anticipatory knowledge of the future of God which inspires them to a genuine hope for a real future for themselves and all creation. This vision of hope, in turn, establishes them in a state of conflict with the present reality which is "not yet" the realization of the promised future. This hope-filled existence in "contradiction" to what "already is" moves believers to "revolution" —or, more accurately, to "provolution" toward a new future—by means of a self-emptying love directed toward the world and on its behalf, precisely because this world is destined for the "better promises" of God. Out of their faith-inspired and hope-freed love, Christians derive a willingness to suffer the burdens of the present creation so as to do their part in leading it toward that new future which is already "coming." Thus, the efforts exerted under the "cross of the present" are an attempt at moving present creation into conformity with what is promised to it. In this way the struggle of Christians is "to bring the present into **correspondence** with the arriving future."[41] And yet, Moltmann always remains convinced that we can "have" neither God nor his future, but can only await them in "active hope" for the duration of our "existence in exodus."[42]

The creative presence of the coming God has the effect of opening up history, but this openness is as yet neither absolute nor completed; it is an eschatological openness, which means that for those who are summoned into the divine covenant, their experience and their expectations of history are "both opened up and tied down" by the future promises of the God they believe.[43] This dual function of the divine promises is derived from the fact that they contain within themselves both gospel and command. In Moltmann's analysis, "the people of God" are so designated by virtue of their having been chosen to enter into a "history of promise" which alters the meaning and purpose of their existence. Since the revelation-event involves "election, covenant, promise and mission," at one and the same time believers are both invited and guided into the new future of God.[44] There is both a liberating and a shaping element to the hope which is the gift of God's promises, because in addition to being inspired and encouraged by these promises, believers come to know also that at least certain things—the prohibitions of the divine commands—shall not work, either for the fulfillment of God's promises, or for the completion of the mission of God's people.

Because there is an "interval of tension" between the issuance of the promises of God and the time of their fulfillment, an "historic process" is begun which affords people the "freedom for obedience." If believers wish to share in the promised fulfillment, they must "arise and go to the place to which the promise points." This means, in effect, that the promises of God are not only indicative, but also directive. "Promise and command, the pointing of the goal and the pointing of the way, therefore belong immediately together." There is thus a judicial character to the promises, which means that the "people of election" to whom these promises are addressed, now find themselves in a covenantal relationship with God whose fidelity is assured, but whose faithfulness also establishes a history that requires obedience. What is commanded (**gebietet**) is what the promise offers (**bietet**)—the love of God. Thus Moltmann observes that "the commandments of the covenant, which point our hopes in the promise to the path of physical obedience, are nothing else but the ethical reverse of the promise itself. The promised life here appears as the life that is commanded."[45]

And yet this exhortative and challenging dimension of God's promise does not carry the strict legal connotation of "law" understood in the sense of rigid and "abstract norms of ideal orders that always exist and reflect their images in time." The commandments, in fact, have "just as much a future tenor as the promises" in which

103

they, along with the gospel, are grounded. Obedience in the context of faith is always "the fruit of hope." As to the relationship existing between the promise of God and the obedience of human beings, there is no question but that "in essence a divine promise itself contains the power of its fulfillment in the faithfulness and might of the God who promises." Thus when Moltmann proposes that the fruit of Christianity's promise-inspired hope must be an active and suffering obedience, he does not mean to suggest his adherence to any theory which would attempt to portray the fulfillment of the promises as in any way dependent upon human obedience.

Even the idea that Christian obedience might serve "as the occasion for the fulfillment by God himself" of his promises receives no sympathy from Moltmann, who rejects as humanistic or "activistic messianism" the view expressed by Martin Buber to the effect that " 'the redemption of the world is left to the power of our conversion. God has no wish for any other means of perfecting his creation than by our help. He will not reveal his kingdom until we have laid its foundations'."[46] That God desires and, in fact, requires human assistance in preparation of his kingdom's full appearance, is, as we saw in the previous chapter, a major point in Teilhard's theology. Thus, on this issue Moltmann clearly stands in opposition not only to Buber, but also to Teilhard. Later in this study we will consider further this point of difference between Moltmann and Teilhard.

Moltmann's position on the role of obedience in the lives of the covenantal people is derived in large part from the work of Gerhard von Rad, who argues that in the Old Testament, God's revelation comes to be known by Israel partly as prevenient grace and partly as a demand upon her. Yet Israel's relationship to Yahweh is definitely not a "legal" one, if this term is taken to mean that the relationship can only be maintained "by the rendering of particular obedience," for Israel's election preceded, not only her reception of the commandments, but also any opportunity for her proving her obedience.[47] Von Rad does maintain, however, that by Yahweh's proclamation in the Decalogue of his sovereign rights over Israel, and in Israel's recognition and acceptance of the binding character of the specific ordinances, the election of Israel is put into effect and her appropriation and conveyance to Yahweh is completed.[48]

While the commandments represent no absolute moral law in any full sense, they do embody Yahweh's offer of life, and place the

Israelites in the position of having to decide for life or for death. But it is von Rad's insistence, that these commandments are not prefixed to the covenant in any conditional sense "as if the covenant would only come into effect once obedience had been rendered." Rather, the reverse is the case: the covenant is made, and with it the revelation of the commandments is received (Dt. 27:9-10).[49] Following von Rad, Moltmann translates the Old Testament commandments into an exclusively hortatory mood, thereby distinguishing them from both the indicative mood of the gospel and from the imperative mood of the law. In this context, the message of salvation already received is never called into question, and with regard to the inner motivation for keeping the commandments, it is suggested simply that "love for Yahweh and thankfulness to him will lead Israel into obedience."[50]

Against both von Rad and Moltmann it might be argued that it is one thing to insist that the covenant is inaugurated prior to, and maintained apart from, Israel's obedience to the commandments. It is quite another thing, however, to argue that the covenant will be completed, and its promises fulfilled, wihout obedience. Indeed, in Moses' address to the Israelites, there appears to be no hesitation in his understanding that obedience is a condition which must be met before the fulfillment of Yahweh's promises may be reasonably expected: "If you will obey the Lord your God by diligently observing all his commandments which I lay upon you this day, then the Lord your God will raise you high above all nations of the earth, and all these blessings shall come to you and light upon you, because you obey the Lord your God" (Dt. 28:1-2). The difficulty lies, however, in exactly defining the status or nature of the condition of obedience.

To deny that obedience is sufficient for participation in the kingdom is understandable, but to deny that obedience, or at least a lack of disobedience, is a prerequisite for the kingdom is not a responsible position; in effect, it makes God's bestowal and establishment of the kingdom simply and totally an arbitrary decision, rather than a loving one. What is perpetrated here is a double act of injustice, for it deprives God of the freedom to establish the kind of economy in which the efforts of human beings are seen as truly praiseworthy, significant, and even integral to the designs of God; further, it robs human beings of any sense of urgency to continue the struggle by means of which the approach of the kingdom is hastened, and thus it plants the seed of human irresponsibility.

If von Rad and Moltmann are intent simply upon breaking the mold which holds Old Testament theology to a strict legalism where the law is confining and deadening, their reflections are most pertinent and helpful; to the extent, however, that they deny a place for the positive contribution which loving and responsive obedience, as opposed to obedience in fear and trembling, may make toward the appearance of the kingdom, their efforts become self-defeating. Obviously, the law cannot effect salvation; neither, of course, can obedience, but the latter, I suggest, should and does serve at least as an occasion for the complete fulfillment of the promises by God. The truth of the matter, finally, is that Moltmann's thinking about the meaning and role of Christian obedience is somewhat difficult to determine in any precise way. How is this the case?

Moltmann speaks often and forcefully of the mission of Christianity; he does not hesitate to suggest that Christians must make themselves known in their productive obedience or creative discipleship, whereby they respond to the promises of God through their struggle for the future of freedom in society, and for the wholeness of the new humanity. Somehow persons of Christian obedience are to participate in the future's "process of coming" through their efforts to realize this future in historical foreshadowings. Following the lead of Johannes Metz, Moltmann goes so far as to speak of Christian eschatology and hope as being not simply receptive and passive but, rather, active, productive, and militant. Thus Christians are "construction workers" of the future and " 'co-workers' of the promised kingdom of God and its universal peace and its righteousness."[51]

In the construction of the future it is not unthinkable that individual nations and societies should regard themselves "as transitions on the way to a common organized humanity;" to this end, loyalty to one's own class, race, or nation must yield to that solidarity with others which is necessary for overcoming "common economic and military world crises." Moltmann tirelessly exhorts Christians to strike a creative and harmonious balance between prayer and worldly involvement, between contemplation and political struggle, and between the vertically-directed transcendental religion of faith and the horizontally-directed religion of solidarity with others in love. For Moltmann, there is simply no way to approach the risen Christ if we do not move toward solidarity with those whom he came to free and for whom he died.[52] Clearly, Moltmann would maintain that Christians who have true faith necessarily and naturally live in hope and are inspired, encouraged and directed to the labors of love.

Thus, although the kingdom of God belongs to the future of God, Moltmann knows that the kingdom does "not simply lie in readiness in the future," but is given rather to those who work and search for it: "No one will see the land of fulfillment if he does not start seeking it."[53] Insofar as it develops within the atmosphere of God's covenantal promise which is both gospel and command, Christian hope must necessarily be responsible; it must take shape in a creative obedience. It must, as Moltmann indicates, "become a commitment to the future as it seizes and realizes, in obedience and anticipated joy, the open possibilities in the world process . . . In the expectation of Christ's coming, it performs now whatever makes straight the way of the Lord."[54] Christian life, then, is an "eschatological practice" determined by the God of the future and not by any fixed natural order.[55] Joined to the God who promises to make all things new, the exodus community of faith labors in hope and in love to change the world "in the expectation of the divine change."[56] There is no way in which believing hope can justify itself as a passive resignation, a "quietistic trust," or a "form of escapism which attempts no remedy for the present misery."[57]

But there is another side to Moltmann's thought. For all his emphasis on a militant responsibility for the future, he nonetheless insists that the object of Christian hope is always the promise of God, which is embraced and anticipated in a confidence that relies on the fidelity of the God "who raises the dead and calls into being the things that are not" (Rom. 4:17). What moves the believer, then, is the "God of hope" (Rom. 15:13), the **Deus spei**, and not the god, hope, the **Deus spes** of Ernst Bloch.[58] This means that the new future of the "realm of freedom" can never be simply the result of the "realm of work and necessity," but appears rather as both "the coming redemption from coercions and necessities under which we must act in the present" and as "goal of the human striving, as absolution in forgiveness of sins and as goal of new obedience." The new future of God is the present force of Christian mobilization, but it is also always the gift freely given.[59]

The situation is this, then. Moltmann may indeed speak of believers as construction workers of the future and as "co-workers" of the promised kingdom, but it remains problematic as to what real validity and effectiveness their co-operation has. Moltmann is sure that "it would be impossible to anticipate the future if the future were not coming toward us." More specifically, Moltmann maintains the position that "the real future is not identical with the successes of our activity" and that it is only because this future comes toward us, that our human activities are not in vain (1 Cor. 15:58).[60]

In these views Moltmann does not differ significantly from that other theologian of hope, Teilhard de Chardin. Where he does differ significantly, however, and where he seems to empty the concept of believers as "co-workers" for the new future of any meaningful content, is in his argument that Christian labor out of loving and grateful obedience serves not even as the occasion for God's fulfillment of his promises. If Moltmann's position is correct, then what meaning and power can be attached to such phrases as "productive obedience," "creative discipleship," "productive and militant hope?" What really is produced or created by individuals of Christian hope? Moltmann does indeed expect Christians to be loving of God and grateful to him, and to embody this love and gratitude in creative efforts to overcome human suffering and oppression. He does not make clear, however, what the outcome of this Christian labor is, nor the precise nature of the relationship between the results of Christian involvement in history and the fulfillment of God's promise in the full appearance of his kingdom.

We must argue that the action of Christians is admittedly responsive to the word and work of God; but it is not simply a reactive process. Furthermore, there is a way in which Christian activity is creative without, however, being autocratic and autonomous. Within the atmosphere of love which God has provided for the development of man, human activity is co-creative, so that both human individuality and divine uniqueness are preserved, but need not be defensively guarded. In the recognition and surrender of mutual love, defenses only serve to hurt and to hide. In his zeal to do justice to God's sovereignty, Moltmann, it seems, underestimates both God and human beings. In refusing to allow God to be fully a God of love who needs humanity's labor because he loves human beings, Moltmann, I suggest, not only sets limitations to the wisdom and graciousness of God, but succeeds also in refusing to allow individuals to become fully human through responsive and truly creative participation with God in the preparation of the new future.

Summary Reflections: Teilhard and Moltmann

The best way perhaps to summarize the general movement of Moltmann's ethical reflections is to compare and contrast the structure and motivation of his theological endeavor with the work of Teilhard. In Teilhard's theology the social and cosmic implications of morality are revealed as truly intrinsic to the human struggle for continued involvement in the redemptive work of Christ. Moreover, the establishment of hope in the cosmic Christ of evolution, who is still in the process of formation, transforms the cast of moral considerations. The effort now is to build up the earth and hasten the approach of the one who is to come; no longer do human beings suffer to recapture what was lost—the innocence of a primitive Adam. Teilhard's attention to the truly cosmic dimensions of Christian hope makes his ethical reflections especially pertinent in dealing with ecological-environmental questions. The world-encompassing "vision of hope" which Teilhard is able to maintain cannot be explained by saying, as Moltmann does, that Teilhard's eschatology is linked to nature, while Moltmann, by contrast, links eschatology to history.[61] The truth, rather, lies in the fact that by linking eschatology primarily with human beings who are creatures both of history and of nature, Teilhard is able to indicate the basis for his expectation of the eschatological transformation of both society and the earth.

With regard to the historical transformation of politics and society, Moltmann may indeed speak more radically than Teilhard, but I suggest that even in this area Teilhard, by taking seriously the contribution of Christian involvement in fostering the spiritualization of the universe, stirs up a greater sense of immediacy and urgency in people than Moltmann does. My reason for saying this is that Teilhard is convinced, as we have seen, of the necessity of humanity's real co-operation with God in the preparation of the new future. Whatever else Teilhard may be, he is not a naive optimist who fails to reckon with the power of present evil; thus the glow surrounding the Omega Point is powerless to reduce him to an attitude of eschatological frivolity, which fails to recognize the need for both long-and-short-term planning with regard to the future.

As human beings we build the earth so that God may build his kingdom among us; all the while, however, the first undertaking is the real foundation of the second, even though it always remains subject to and awaits its final transformation by the Lord of heaven and earth. Through his insistence upon the need for God's trans-formation of our work, Teilhard intends to preserve both the sovereignty of God and the graciousness of his dealing with us. Finally, for Teilhard, the phenomenon of Christian hope avoids a teleological determinism, because the continued progress of evolution depends upon our increasing freedom to recognize and respond to our personal and social obligations. The history of salvation, then, is not simply an extension of natural history; there is always recognition both of the grace of God and of the sin and guilt of humanity.

As for Moltmann, his concern is with the development of a political theology, or what he calls "a new ethic of the hope of faith," in which the historical progressivism of liberal theology is held in check by an emphasis upon the sovereignty of God and a vital theology of the cross.[62] Between the cross and the resurrection, between the suffering of the present and the glory of a new future, there is only the bridge of God's divine **creatio ex nihilo**. By analyzing eschatology in terms of history, Moltmann succeeds in finding a basis for socio-political involvements of a "provolutionary" nature but, to my mind, his theology would be enhanced were it to entertain more seriously and effectively the possibility of a positive contribution which human beings may make to the work of God. His insistence is always that both the promise of God and the fulfillment of that promise are gifts freely given, and as such may never be made dependent in any way upon the obedience of humanity. And yet, of course, grateful and loving labor is expected of us, for without it we have no reason to hope for the fulfillment of the divine promise.

Through our active response to God, we strive to bring the present into correspondence with the promised future; our work, then, is one of anticipation, but if it serves not even as an occasion for the fulfillment by God of his promise, our accomplishments, it seems, are put in jeopardy. We may thus seriously question whether Moltmann, for all his deference to revisionary Marxist theory, has really been moved by its critique of Christianity, or whether he has seriously met its challenge by providing people with a real incentive to hope for all things, including the works of their hands and of their minds. If human involvement in history is demanded while the works of men and women are not necessary to the fulfillment of the new future, then Moltmann must explain in what sense the believer's hope can be creative, productive and militant. As far as I can see, this explanation is not forthcoming.

Both Teilhard and Moltmann see Christian hope as an inspiration to loving and obedient service. Out of this hope, Teilhard, on the one hand, proposes an ethics of human conquest and of co-operative creation with God whereby an individual's labor provides a "preliminary sketch" for the repletive work of God in building up his kingdom. It is an instance of human involvement in the kingdom's creation through co-operation with God. Moltmann, on the other hand, outlines an ethics in which a believer tries to make the future of God present through a process of "anticipation by correspondence." The believer, that is, tries to anticipate or approximate the quality of life in God's future by presently living in correspondence with it insofar as it has been revealed and embodied in the life and teaching of Jesus Christ. But for neither Teilhard nor Moltmann is the kingdom of God simply a creation by human beings; it is always the object of God's promise and of humanity's active hope.

As gospel, the promise of God provides us with a new history and a new future, the effect of which is to challenge us in our ethical reflections never to canonize the status quo, never to stand passively before the obvious incompatibility between the quality of life characterizing today's world and the quality of life offered in God's promised future. As command, however, the promise of God reminds us that in our movement into the future, not every kind of involvement is expected of us nor allowed us. Together, then, promise as gospel and promise as command work to make the ethical mode of Christian existence one of "expectant creativity."

We shall look at this notion of "expectant creativity" more closely in our concluding chapter where we will also continue our comparative analysis of Teilhard and Moltmann. For now, I will suggest simply that in Teilhard's theology the emphasis is on creativity, whereas in Moltmann's thinking it is on expectation. But what I shall refer to as Teilhard's theory of "co-operative creation" or "creation through co-operation" allows more room for expectation than Moltmann's theory of "anticipatory correspondence" or "anticipation by correspondence" will allow for perduring human creativity; I think this is so, moreover, despite the fact that Moltmann does not hesitate to speak of "creative love" or "creative discipleship" as the only attitude in our open-ended history which can constitute "the appropriate counterpart to that which is promised and is to come."[63]

111

All of Moltmann's involvement in the dialogue with Marxist theorists has only served to increase his scepticism with regard to any "social gospel" movement which would try to equate the growth and development of God's new future with the ethical and spiritual progress of humanity. It is quite clear that for him the new future is always a predicate of God as promise, and never a predicate of society as progressive process.[64] It is fine, of course, to insist that the new future is always a matter of hoping rather than of seeing, a matter, in other words, of the **coming** of the kingdom rather than of the **becoming** of the world; nonetheless, if the work of human obedience and activity has no effect, either in hastening the arrival of the kingdom, or in forestalling its establishment, we can only conclude that the labors of men and women lack lasting significance in the eyes of God. And if divine significance is not attached to the accomplishments of human beings, we must seriously question whether human achievements have any lasting significance for individuals themselves. If they do not, then really we have nothing to motivate ourselves, nothing to be responsible for, and hence nothing to hope for actively.

CHAPTER IV

REFERENCES

1. Jürgen Moltmann, Religion, Revolution, and The Future, trans. M. Douglas Meeks (New York: Charles Scribner's Sons, 1969), pp. 95-98.

2. Ibid., p. 20.

3. Vernard Eller, "Comments on An Unsolicited Series," The Christian Century, 85, No. 15 (April 10, 1968), 459-60.

4. Jürgen Moltmann, Theology of Hope, trans. James W. Leitch (New York: Harper & Row, 1967), pp. 42, 44, 143.

5. Ibid., pp. 126, 129-30.

6. Ibid., pp. 102-06, 111.

7. Ibid., pp. 103, 107.

8. Moltmann, Religion, p. 8.

9. Ibid., p. 10.

10. Ibid., pp. 202, 208.

11. Ibid., p. 202.

12. Ibid., pp. 28, 216, 29-30.

13. Ibid., pp. 61-2, 34-5.

14. Ibid., pp. 40-1.

15. Ibid., p. 95; also see Daniel L. Migliore, "Biblical Eschatology and Political Hermeneutics," Theology Today, XXVI (1969), 116-32 at 122-23.

16. Migliore, "Biblical Eschatology," pp. 119-21, 128; Moltmann, Religion, p. 14; also see Jürgen Moltmann, "Hoping and Planning," Cross Currents, XVIII, No. 3 (Summer, 1968) 307-18. A modified version of Moltmann's article appears also in his Hope and Planning, trans. Margaret Clarkson (New York: Harper & Row, 1971), pp. 178-99.

17. Ibid., p. 129.

18. Walter H. Capps, "An Assessment of the Theological Side of the School of Hope," Cross Currents, XVIII, No. 3 (Summer, 1968), 319-35 at 331.

19. Moltmann, Religion, p. 41.

20. Moltmann, Theology of Hope, pp. 161, 222; also Martin R. Tripole, S.J., Community As Eschatology: An Investigation of the Theology of the Church of Jürgen Moltmann with A General Introduction to His Thought (Unpublished Doctoral Dissertation: Institut Catholique de Paris, May 1972), pp. 205-06.

21. Moltmann, Religion, pp. 33, 17-8, 51-3; also Theology of Hope, p. 281.

22. Ibid., p. 53. The centrality of the theology of the cross, both for Moltmann's thinking and for all Christian theology, is seen in Moltmann's second major work, The Crucified God (New York: Harper & Row, Publishers, 1974).

23. Ibid., p. 58.

24. Jürgen Moltmann, "Political Theology," in his The Experiment Hope, ed., trans., with foreword by M. Douglas Meeks (Phila.: Fortress Press, 1975), pp. 101-18 at 103, 118; see also George Hunsinger, "The Crucified God and the Political Theology of Violence: A Critical Survey of Jürgen Moltmann's Recent Thought: I," The Heythrop Journal, XIV, No. 3 (July, 1973), 266-79.

25. Moltmann, Religion, p. 218; also Theology of Hope, pp. 20, 33-4.

26. Ibid., pp. 122, 127-128.

27. Ibid., pp. 120, 117.

28. Ibid., p. 140.

29. Ibid., p. 121.

30. Ibid., p. 79.

31. Ibid., p. 146.

32. Ibid., p. 135; Tripole, Community as Eschatology, p. 191.

33. Ibid., pp. 32, 129.

34. Ibid., p. 17.

35. Ibid., pp. 143-45.

36. The material in this and the preceding paragraph is from Jürgen Moltmann, "Racism and the Right to Resist," The Hope Experiment, pp. 131-46 at 142-43. He takes the phrase "more irredeemable guilt" from D. Bonhoeffer, Ethics, ed. E. Bethge (New York: Macmillan, 1965), p. 241. Moltmann's views on violence and love are treated by George Hunsinger, "The Crucified God and the Political Theology of Violence: A Critical Survey of Jürgen Moltmann's Recent Thought: II," The Heythrop Journal, XIV, No. 4 (Oct., 1973), 379-95 at 387 ff.

37. Moltmann, Hope and Planning, p. 129 n. 44.

38. Ibid., pp. 172-73.

39. Hunsinger observes that in his treatment of violence, Moltmann acknowledges the cross as a formal principle but not as a material one. Consequently, he judges that Moltmann is too quick to allow violent resistance to injustice. See "Crucified God and Political Theology of Violence: II," pp. 393-95.

40. Moltmann, Religion, p. 147.

41. Tripole, Community as Eschatology, p. 256, n. 313.

42. Moltmann, Theology of Hope, p. 16.

43. Ibid., p. 290.

44. Ibid., p. 112.

45. Ibid., pp. 120-21.

46. Ibid., pp. 122-24. Moltmann refers to Martin Buber, Gog und Magog, 1949, p. 297 and to H. J. Kraus, "Gespräch mit M. Buber," Evangelische Theologie, 12, 1952, pp. 76 ff.

47. Gerhard von Rad, Old Testament Theology, trans. D.M.G. Stalker, 2 vols., (New York: Harper & Row, 1962, 1965), II, pp. 389-91.

48. Ibid., I, p. 192.

49. Ibid., I, pp. 193-94.

50. Ibid., II, p. 393; I, p. 199.

51. Jürgen Moltmann, "Theology as Eschatology," The Future of Hope. Theology as Eschatology, ed. Frederick Herzog (New York: Herder & Herder, 1970) pp. 1-50 at 45-6. Moltmann here acknowledges his indebtedness to Johannes B. Metz, "Schöpferische Eschatologie," Orientierung, XXX, No. 9 (May 15, 1966), 107-09. Also see Moltmann, Religion, pp. 217-18.

52. Jürgen Moltmann, The Church in the Power of the Spirit, trans. Margaret Kohl (New York: Harper & Row, 1977), pp. 180-81; 282-88.

53. Moltmann, Religion, pp. 217, 210.

54. Moltmann, "Hope without Faith: An Eschatological Humanism without God," Is God Dead? Concilium Series, vol. 16, ed. Johannes B. Metz (New York: Paulist Press, 1966), pp. 25-40 at 34.

55. Gerald G. O'Collins, S.J., "Spes Quaerens Intellectum," Interpretation, 22, No. 1 (Jan., 1968), 36-52 at 48.

56. Moltmann, Theology of Hope, pp. 304, 84.

57. Gerald G. O'Collins, S.J., "The Principle and Theology of Hope," Scottish Journal of Theology, 21, 2 (1968), p. 139; also see Moltmann, Theology of Hope, pp. 325-38.

58. Moltmann, Religion, p. 158.

59. Moltmann, "Theology as Eschatology," p. 50.

60. Ibid., p. 48.

61. Walter H. Copps, Time Invades the Cathedral. Tensions in the School of Hope (Phila.: Fortress Press, 1972), p. 137.

62. Moltmann, Religion, p. 218.

63. Moltmann, Theology of Hope, pp. 334-35.

64. See Carl E. Braaten, "American Historical Experience and Christian Reflection," Projections: Shaping an American Theology for the Future, eds. Thomas F. O'Meara and Donald M. Weisser (Garden City, New York: Doubleday Image Books, 1970), pp. 93-115 at 100.

CHAPTER V
EXPECTANT CREATIVITY:
THE ETHICAL MODE OF CHRISTIAN EXISTENCE

Introduction

As we reach the last stage of our study, it may help to highlight the various steps we have taken in the course of our investigation. The intention all along has been to expose the dynamism of Christian hope as an anthropological and theological dimension in the effort at ethical reflection. After arguing in chapter one for the essentially eschatological orientation of Christian ethics, and hence for the appearance of hope as its central driving-force, some indication was given in chapter two of the character of hope, of the foundation of Christian hope in faith, and of hope's relationship to Christian love. Then in chapters three and four an exploration was made into the general contours of the theological frameworks of Teilhard and Moltmann with the intention of discovering how the dynamism of hope permeates and enlivens their theologies, and thus provides a context for their ethical reflections. What we want to indicate now in a more integrated and systematic fashion is how Christian hope comes to bear in a formal way upon the ethical enterprise. To do this, we will look once again at the theological structures of Teilhard and Moltmann, and then a broader discussion will be initiated in which questions will be confronted regarding the relevancy of an ethics of hope, hope's relationship to love, and the requirements of a methodology for an adequate ethics of hope.

Christian Involvement:
"Co-operative Creation" or "Anticipatory Correspondence?"

In Teilhard's theology there is no room either for a detachment which is really a timidity to fight or for a resignation that is a failure to struggle. He is convinced that fundamentally there is no contradiction between true personal development and spiritual growth. Thus, the more Christian action is never a less human act. And yet, in Teilhard's world a mature spirituality or ethical discipline displays two integrated movements: "a passion for activity—for God; a passion for passivity—because of God."[1] Through their faith and hope in the power of Christ to attract and to perfect in personal union all those who believe in him, Christians are stirred to a renewed interest in, and commitment to, the mission entrusted to them of fulfilling the human race, constructing the world, and laying the foundations of the Parousia. In light of an intimate connection between Christ's victory and the constructs of human endeavor, Teilhard believes that both the natural and the supernatural orders are still in the process of completion. And so, while it is indeed the role of the supernatural to transform "nature," nevertheless, "it cannot do so apart from the matter which nature provides it with." Thus, it is the belief and hope of Christians that in building up the earth, they are at the same time preparing the world for its final glorious transformation and laying the foundations for the ultimate perfection and fulfillment of God's promised future.[2]

Insofar as Teilhard envisions the natural elements of human endeavor as absolutely necessary to providing the work of salvation "with its fuel and with a suitable material," and insofar as he further contends that "the supernatural fullness of Christ depends upon the natural fullness of the world," Christians are encouraged to establish a relationship to the world that embodies elements both of attachment and detachment.[3] Their struggle is to remake all that is presently in the world, while at the same time restraining themselves— out of hope, the convictions of faith, and the demands of love—in order to bear witness to the expected and awaited completion of the earth, which is already in progress through the initiative of the divine transformation. Thus, Christians labor in love to shape and conquer the world, without forgetting, however, the promise of an escape from it into the future. They must assist, then, in forging a pathway out of the present, while remembering always that their ultimate goal, and that of the universe, is achieved finally in and through Christ-Omega.[4] Precisely because of their hope in Christ the Evolver, Christians refuse to allow themselves to be so dominated by matter, or by their own activity, that their nascent union with God would suffer.

Teilhard has often been accused, of course, of failing to distinguish clearly enough between the created order and the order of grace. The exact point where reason stops and faith begins, or where phenomenology ceases and theology arises, is left undetermined. And yet in explaining the relationship between the end of time, history's immanent conclusion, and the second coming of Christ in the Parousia,

Teilhard clearly maintains that the former event is only the occasion of the latter one, but not its cause. Thus in no way does Teilhard naively confuse the human phenomenon with the divine one.

Christians must await the establishment of the new future by God, while God is pleased to await this future's human preparation as believers attend to the building of the earth and the development of a world-community, which is consciously sought in faith under the auspices of hope and through the energies of love. Teilhard, then, is neither a material reductionist who is blind to the reality of God's offering of his life in grace, nor a spiritualist who ridicules the obstinacies of nature. Rather, he is a transformationist who understands that with the right intention, and in union with Christ, all nature is amenable to the transfiguring process by means of which the Pleroma is inaugurated.

Within this context, Christian love is the willingness to accept and to affirm the liberty and dignity of all human beings, and to labor in the establishment of an atmosphere which is conducive to the development of their human potential. Precisely as such, love demands and implies a belief in the future of humanity, and a hope which is associated with that future. This hope calls Christians to a love that labors to embody itself in a human union, which is collective of the energies of human beings, but which also personalizes, differentiates and, hence, creates with greater intensity the identity and value of the individual. Thus, what is most indicative and expressive of the liberating and creative energy of hope is the impelling motivation it lends to Christian love.

In turning to Moltmann we enter a different, more traditional, realm of theological discourse. For him, revelation, which is recognized and accepted as promise and embraced in hope, at once opens up a pathway for history, and requires that in their movement forward, believers must develop a "missionary enterprise and the responsible exercise of hope, accepting the suffering that is involved in the contradiction of [present] reality, and setting out towards the promised future;" in the final analysis this promised future appears in its fulfillment as "the end of death, and a new creation in which amid the life and righteousness of all things God is all in all."[5] In this context the nature of humanity is clearly portrayed as eschatological in that its meaning and fulfillment are revealed only in the future of that history which is given to us in light of our divine mission. Thus, as Moltmann recognizes, the anthropological question of self-identity can be answered only in the face of our call and the mission entrusted to us by God. Our questions, then, about ourselves and human nature are answered finally in God's response: "I will be with you;" thus, "the **natura hominis** first emerges from the **forma futurae vitae**." To the extent that we hope in the new creation promised by God, we are presently "in **statu nascendi**," that is, we are in the process of being brought into being "by the calling, coaxing, compelling word of God."[6]

Precisely insofar as no ethics has human significance in isolation from its anthropological context, we must now go a step further than Moltmann and suggest that not only the anthropological question, but also the ethical one, must be conceived and answered in light of the "**forma futurae vitae**." For this reason, then, every determination of the ethical good should also be made in relation to the divine promise: "I will be with you." Accordingly, what Moltmann says of the encouraging and compelling word of God can be said too of the ethical good: "it is an earnest of things to come, and binds us to itself in order to point and direct us to greater things." This ethical good, moreover, which is pursued in hope in much the same way as the word of promise is heard in hope, can finally be attained by means of a dialectical tension in which what is good is both confidently awaited and wholeheartedly sought.[7]

In relation to Moltmann's theology, Teilhard's thinking is marked by a more earthly sensitivity which moves him to take history and the historical process seriously as the necessary preparation for the eschaton, so that in a real sense the end is conditioned and shaped by our earth-building activities undertaken and carried on in faith. Throughout his life and work, Teilhard struggled to overcome humanism's charge that Christianity was otherworldly, and it was his effort in this regard which led him to deny Christians the privilege and leisure of leaping over history in order to attain to the end prematurely. Rather, the pathway to the eschaton is through history and the world.

What is especially inspiring is Teilhard's suggestion that the results of our human efforts in history will not be lost, annihilated or cast aside by God when his kingdom is fully established. Rather, under the transforming, transfiguring touch of God, the works of our faith will remain as eternal signs of our affirmative reply to God's invitation to share his life and to enter into co-operative creation with him in the building of a new future. As with Teilhard, so also with Moltmann, I am sure, the intention is to encourage "a socially serious ethic of historical responsibility," but Moltmann, even more so than Teilhard, is unable to articulate fully the precise dimensions of the dialectical relationship between God's present promise and future gift and humanity's historical response in either hopeful activity or hopeless inactivity.[8]

It may be said that for Teilhard, at least, the historical attainment of the end of the world in unity is the occasion for the divine enactment of the Parousia in the glory of its fulfillment; in contrast to this, the most that may be said with regard to Moltmann, is that for him history is the arena in which we are expected to respond to the promises of God in an attitude of love, in anticipation of the establishment or fulfillment by God of the new future, and as a symbolic expression of our desire to hasten the approach of the **novum ultimum** by attempting always to make the present over into greater correspondence with the future as promised. But it remains unclear in Moltmann's thinking as to what fate awaits the fruits of our labors. Shall they be taken up, transformed, and authentically consummated, and if so, why? Or shall they be forgotten, cast out, and catastrophically dissolved like entropized matter? If the former is the case, it ought to be indicative, as Teilhard suggests, of the essential, even though provisional, functional value of our human effort, and of the legitimacy of this effort's plea for divine acknowledgment;[9] but this is a possibility which Moltmann apparently has difficulty in accepting. And if the latter alternative, the dissolution and ultimate ineffectualness of our efforts, characterizes the lot of human productivity and creativity, then really in no way is the new future either the future of this world or our future. And even more appalling and disheartening is the realization that this new future would now take form, not as the gift of a loving God who is appreciative of the obedient faith and hope-filled love of his people in response to his promises as gospel and command, but rather as the arbitrary expression of the will of some whimsical demon.

It goes without saying that a truly adequate view of the Christian future must effectively balance polar statements. Thus, the new future is not the result of complex extrapolations from past and present trends, and consequently it cannot be simply manipulated and domesticated; but at the same time, this future may not be so idealized and isolated that it is no longer recognizable as the real future of human beings and their earth. Moreover, our acknowledgment in faith and hope that the future is God's future over which he has final dominion must not be allowed to obscure the fact that this same future is also our future for which we bear responsibility. Finally, insofar as the future is appreciated as the critical point of reference with regard to the past and present, it is precisely the power by means of which we are enabled to build a new world. In this sense, then, the future is not an instrument simply of self-negation and world-denial, which is wielded solely to reject the present and the past. The future, rather, calls us to come to terms with history in such a way that the sins and pathologies of the past and the present will never be repeated.[10]

In contrast to teleological thinking which is convinced that the future history of humanity always lies in perfect continuity with the potential of our natural resources, the Christian eschatology of both Teilhard and Moltmann stakes its own existence and the very meaning of humanity on the expectation of something truly "new," of something that has never been, so that the future is not simply a correlative or projection of human natural potential. And yet, the eschatological context of Christian faith, hope and love, far from excluding temporal involvement in the affairs of history, actually implies such commitment as an expression of our recognition and acceptance of the social bonds which have been established among people in light of God's promises, especially as these have been incarnated in the life and work of Christ.[11]

Although Teilhard's theological writings have a strong scriptural undercurrent, as is evident in the pervasive power which the Pauline concept of the "recapitulation" of all things in Christ (Eph. 1:10) wields in the structuring of his theology, the relative paucity of specific biblical terms, especially those of Old Testament origin, is a reflection of Roman Catholic theological methods, emphases, and inadequacies in the days of Teilhard's training.[12] There is no question but that some development of the covenant theme, for instance, would have complemented his theory of history as a preparation for the Pleroma, and would have lent encouragement to the believer's struggle to assist in creating a world of greater and more visible unanimity. Nevertheless, by challenging people to prepare here and now for God's new future, Teilhard still manages to restrain Christians from finding any solace in a morality devoid of active and effective involvement in social, economic and political efforts at building a better community.

Teilhard's hope is always to effect a rejuvenation of Christianity so as to make it the force it must be in order to soothe modern man's outrage of conscience over religion's ineffectualness in the world. This is an ambition which Moltmann also entertains, but whereas Teilhard envisions Christian involvement in history as a real and lasting preparation for the eschaton through a process of co-operative creation with God, Moltmann is led to view the Christian mission solely as existence in a kind of anticipatory correspondence to the promised future. Moreover, in light of Moltmann's assessment of the status of human obedience in faith, it can only be said that his theological system reduces the possibility, degree, and nature of our real or permanent contribution to the new future to a level which is problematic at best.

Responding to an Outrage of Conscience

The significance of the movement of hope as it has developed in the thinking of Teilhard, Moltmann and others, lies not only in its sound and imaginative theological foundations, but also in its recognition of some legitimate needs and aspirations of human nature which theology for too long had neglected to take seriously. In one form or another, the perennial requirement, as well as the recurring crisis, of Christian theology, and especially of Christian ethics, is to maintain its critical reflection upon the continuing divine-human encounter in such a way as to be able to communicate its insights effectively and with meaning. The success of such an enterprise demands not only an existence sustained by the atmosphere of faith, but also a life nourished by an intelligent relationship to the culture of the times and by a thoughtful appraisal of the meaning of human existence. Theological ethics, then, is a Janus-faced under- taking which closes its eyes either to God, or to humanity and its cultural involvements, only at the price of its own validity and relevance.

There are doubtlessly many ways in which this dual concern of theological ethics, together with its resulting tensions, might be expressed, but for a long time now the most telling criticism against both theology and ethics has come, not from the ranks of those who find their intelligence insulted by theological palaver, but rather from those whose consciences will no longer allow them the peace of silence in the face of the world's injustices. I have in mind such men as Feuerbach, Marx, Nietzsche and, more recently, Ernst Bloch and others who subscribe to the general Marxist critique of religion. It was Nietzsche who expressed the spirit of this criticism quite pithily when he said that "it is no longer our reason, but our taste that decides about Christianity." And over fifty years ago Reinhold Niebuhr, who at the time was much taken up with the Marxist philosophy, gave eloquent, even if unheeded, recognition to the problem facing religion and theology:

> The fact is that more men in our modern era are irreligious because religion has failed to make civilization ethical than because it has failed to maintain its intellectual respectability. For every person who disavows religion because some ancient and unrevised dogma outrages his intelligence, several become irreligious because the social impotence of religion outrages their conscience.[13]

To speak of an outrage of conscience indicates that there is at least an implicit expectation that there is no element of Christian faith which ought not to have some implications for Christian living. If this is true in general and in principle, this expectation has only been heightened in our own day. Moreover, there are, as we have seen, theologians like Teilhard and Moltmann who believe that any authentic Christian theology must try to fulfill these expectations. It is the contention of these men that if theology is not to remain at a pre-critical level, then practical or political reason must gain admittance to every theological parley. A new relationship between theory and practice, between knowledge and morality, and between reflection and revolution is being sought in order to determine theological thinking. In this way the classical discussion concerning the relationship between faith and reason finds a new focus in the realm of practical political wisdom, which serves also as a key to the problem of the responsibility of faith that must be active in love.

What especially characterizes the religious consciousness of modern man is the search for the proper expression of those conditions of possibility which embody the good news for the freedom of human beings now and in the future. This search has brought us to the realization that God's relationship to us must be understood in the truly biblical sense, in which we have the room to exercise our power of responsible creativity, the kind of creativity a relationship of love allows and insures. God has given us a role to play in the establishment of the world, and we have come to expect that we will be allowed to labor here in a mature way. This is not to set up human responsibility and freedom as gods, for they can only be false gods and idols. There is, indeed, a kind of freedom which is inhuman, a demon, and a holy terror; it is the kind of freedom which is absolute, and which arises in the atmosphere of loneliness and anonymity, freed from all limitations. It is this very kind of freedom which people are seeking to escape because it breeds death not life, indifference not commitment, and detachment not involvement.

There is another kind of freedom, however, which takes account of the needs and limitations of human nature. It is the freedom which recognizes that we are related to the world and to other people, even to the extent that it is only through our incessant commitment to these relationships that we can be happy and can expect fulfillment. This is a limited freedom but it is human, and it is the kind of freedom which is sacred and demands God's recognition. Our theology of God and of his relationship to us, as well as our view of our personal and social responsibilities, ought, then, never to force us to choose between God and human freedom, or between Christian faith and human creativity. It is because people have had to face this choice, however, that Christian theology is being forced to reconsider what it is about.

The emerging ethics of hope succeeds, I suggest, both in recognizing and in balancing the tension existing between the contrasting but complementary sensibilities of reason and faith. By making use of the past without becoming imprisoned by it, theologians and ethicians of hope are learning to face the past, as well as the present and future, honestly and openly. In a spirit of freedom an ethics of hope calls for responsible participation in the present without encouraging, at the same time, a compulsion to achieve results. Thus, while it views the political scene and the need for justice in a realistic way, and insists that human action is necessary and effective in making a difference in the world, it nevertheless avoids the excesses of political humanism. Moreover, recognizing, as it does, the universal character of the promises of God (Isa. 57:19; Acts. 2:39), an ethics of hope focuses on the common past of believers so as to nourish their common memory and thereby establish a common hope in a common future, the new future of God.[14]

An ethics of hope may be said to embody a liberation of consciousness that might be described as humanity's recovery from its classic failure of nerve in which, consciously or unconsciously, people had been dissuaded from the effort to be wise and good. There is today an increased awareness of what constitutes humanity's work, but this sensitivity is further nuanced for the hopeful believer by an appreciation of what constitutes God's work. The complementary character of the human and divine endeavors is well expressed by Emmanuel Mesthene:

> Man's work is to be wise and good. It is God's work
> to reveal himself to man as wisdom and goodness. It
> is man's work to discern value and to realize possibility. It is God's to be ultimate value and eternal
> possibility, and to imbue man with the grace to know
> and to worship him. It is man's work to know God,
> and God's to be knowable by man. In other words,
> God and man are partners in the work of the world,
> which means at least that man must do his part.[15]

Precisely in the fulfillment of their responsibility to humanity, the world and history, Christians hope to prepare for and anticipate the coming of God's future by means of "a radical involvement in the tasks of the world for the good of mankind." The constant impulse of hope, then, is to embody charity, which is both the law and the fullness of hope. But Christians can love their neighbors as themselves only if they hope for others as they hope for themselves.[16]

A Methodology of Juxtaposition:
Faith in the Past, Hope in the Future, Love in the Present

If, in its reactionary opposition to existentialist theology and situational morality, the ethics of hope were oriented exclusively to the past and the future, it would soon fall victim to debilitating forces, for no enterprise, theological or other, can long survive without engaging itself in the task of expressing the interests and needs of the present. Thus, while theologians of hope often center

128

their attention on those past events in salvation history where God's promises for the future are most clearly evident, there is no intention or desire of absorbing the present into either its past foundations or its future development and fulfillment. As Moltmann himself has insisted, "the new is never totally new" and "the place where the future of men and of the world is decided is the present . . . [which] is the front line of the future."[17] Christopher Mooney likewise observes that an authentic eschatological hope does not disengage Christians from the present, but rather impels them "to view it as the time for decision; not passive dreams for the future but practical initiatives in the present are called for."[18]

Such initiatives are possible for Christians by virtue of the energy which they derive from their promise-inspired vision of a better future and from their hope for this future's realization. Under the light of the eschatological promises, the present limitations of the status quo are felt by Christians as "contrast-experiences" against which they must struggle in a program of creative protest. For Christians, the function and the impact of the gospel, as it bears upon these contrast-experiences, may be explained in two phases, one of pre-reflective reaction, the other, of reflective analysis. In the first phase, the light of the gospel sensitizes Christians to the disparities and inequities of the present situation; to the extent that in this very sensitivity a moral demand for change and improvement arises, concrete moral indicators make their appearance. But it is only in a later stage, when the gospel message matures in a context both of theological reflection and of empirical or scientific analysis of a particular situation, that Christians develop "a responsible and more concrete plan of social and political action."[19]

The theology of hope, inviting believers, as it does, to live in the light of God's **novum ultimum**, expects Christians to live in history with great expectations but without total certainty, for rooted in the view of God as "power of the future" or as the "One who is to come" is an element of mystery. The author of Hebrews knew this well: "By faith Abraham obeyed when he was called to go out to a place which he was to receive as an inheritance; and he went out, not knowing where he was to go" (11:8). This element of hope-filled uncertainty is what enables the dynamism of Christian hope to maintain its unending push toward an absolute future, without which we would have only an ideological design that would prematurely and in an **a priori** way limit and define what is "humanly desirable."[20]

129

Moreover, because of the constant temptation to forget that even the humanly desirable has not yet been fully attained and stands, in fact, in lasting jeopardy, Schillebeeckx's reminder is vitally needed:

> By definition, what has already been achieved is, after all—as is borne out by the constant pressure of eschatological hope—always below the level of the maximum that can be achieved. Pure defense of what has already been achieved, then, would seem . . . to be the basis of those "right-wing" political tendencies which are met with in the case of so many Christians, whatever their denomination may be. But this seems . . . to be an essentially un-Christian interpretation of the Christian faith, which is directed towards the God of our **future**.[21]

Insofar as Christian hope does not completely know the when, or the how, or the final form of its fulfillment, believers must maintain an openness to a future which is "beyond every imaginable human postulate," and also devote their inner energies, as Pieper suggests, "not so much to militantly promoting defined, planned goals and eschatological social aims (in the name of which, all too often, human solidarity is trampled by marching feet)," but rather "to doing daily whatever is prudent, good and just at the time."[22] The truth to be emphasized in Pieper's observation is that the ethics of hope is not a teleological ethics, nor even an exclusively future-facing ethics of love, for the future of God is not simply the as-yet-unrealized effect of the present; rather, this future has entered into the present, thereby filling it with potentiality and offering it a pathway toward fulfillment. An ethics of hope is not concerned exclusively with future consequences, and thus is not reduced entirely to calculating results prudentially in such a way that no judgment can ever be made in the present that an act is unethical and impermissible.

Argumentation in an ethics of hope does not develop in the direction which suggests that the end justifies the means, and yet this ethics is amenable to the proposition that the end determines the human significance and, hence, the morality of the means. When the end is the future of God which comes to us under the form of gospel and of command, the human hope of enjoying that future takes shape necessarily around the form of love, always and everywhere. But the problematic task is to discern the demands of love in a "here and now" that is appreciated as being pregnant with God's promise and as being shaped even now by his redeeming presence.

Piet Fransen has observed that by "living thoroughly in the present we are indeed already living in the future, for only people concerned with real facts and with real people are people of the future. Our future can only be guaranteed by the intensity of our present commitment in faith and charity."[23] By way of comment on Fransen's remark, it must be said that as Christians we do not live "thoroughly" in the present, we are not concerned with "real facts" and with "real people" unless we are deeply sensitive to the "reality-altering" effectiveness of that promise which God made in the past and to whose future fulfillment he remains pledged today. Quite simply we cannot live as Christians of intense faith and charity unless we are also people of intense hope.

It is utterly essential, then, that Christian ethics correctly understand the relationship between the present and the future. Speaking in a different context, Moltmann has posed the question sharply: "Does the present determine the future in extrapolations, or does the future determine the present in anticipations?"[24] Biblically speaking, the answer is clear that the present lies under the influence of the future, for in the life and teaching of Jesus the determinative power of all reality is associated with the future of God's coming kingdom. Thus, although the ethics of hope may never sacrifice the present on the altar of the future in an uncritical way, it must nevertheless provide for what Carl Braaten has described as an "existence in hope toward a future determination of man's essence." It must preserve, in other words, a true history for humanity against the threats, both of an existentialism in which "the future of man's essence is collapsed into the present of his momentary existence," and of an essentialism which sees the future of existence as "but a return to an already fixed essence." An ethics of hope thus believes that the fullness of human nature is eschatological and comes to us from out of the future, so that the totality of its meaning, while rooted in the gift of God's past and present graciousness to us, "is not locked in the structures of what already is or always has been."[25]

In this context Braaten suggests that attempts at an ethical existence must avoid two temptations against hope: one of growing weary of hope, the other of despairing of the future. We yield to the temptation of growing tired of hope "by imagining full satisfaction in the present, relaxing the tension toward the futurity of the promise through the immediacy of false joy and dancing around a stationary god—a golden calf;" we fall to the temptation of despairing of the future "by yearning to return to the past, the land of slavery, the fleshpots of Egypt." In this case the sin of hopelessness makes its appearance in "murmurings in the present, despairing of the promises that point to the future, and desiring to return to the past, even though it means the antihuman security of slavery."[26] In addition to these two forms of hopelessness there are others; we also sin against hope both in the expectation that the future is ours just for the asking, and in the effort to storm the future of God through simple neglect or uncritical destruction of the present and its values.

An ethics of hope must clearly maintain the tradition that the true and full person of the future will not be solely the result of his or her own work, and yet it is inadequate to suggest that an ethics grounded in the eschatological hope of Christianity is simply heteronomous, answerable, that is, to some kind of alien law. Obviously, Christian ethics must move beyond an inquiry only into the nature of humanity and its perfectibility; it must reckon seriously with the fact that here and now we stand under divine scrutiny and thus must face the question as to how the claim of God's future affects our present decisions and conduct.[27] But insofar as the ethics of hope evolves from a divine promise which exists as promise only to the extent that it is received by us in an attitude of hope without, of course, being reducible to that hope, the whole notion of our "pure nature," and hence of any clear and definitive distinction between an "autonomous" and a "heteronomous" ethics, is rendered problematic.

Since our human destiny is itself "supernatural," we must have within ourselves certain "supernatural" conditions of possibility which allow and enable us to receive and acknowledge the promise of the new future which we are led to hope for. Thus, because we are called to hope in light of a promised future, and because our activity ought to be one of creative response to this promise, an eschatologically oriented ethics is most accurately described not as autonomous, self-ruled or teleological; neither is it heteronomous, foreign-ruled or deontological; rather such an ethics is a responsive one of dialogical interaction between the present grace of God and the labor of believing, loving, hoping human beings. The ethics of

Christian hope is unalterably theonomous, subject, that is, to the law of God which happens to be also the internal law of God's people of faith, hope and love.

The fact that Christianity has a future in which to hope, does not, of course, absolve Christians of the need to plan for the future. Not surprisingly, then, the effort at ethical existence will often involve the difficult decision between being either "a political realist hemmed in by societal expectations" or a revolutionary who strives to transform the foundations of the prevailing social and political systems.[28] This decision, in turn, involves the discovery of when and where to draw the line between suffering now for the sake of building a better future, and "brutally sacrificing each generation in favor of the next succeeding and of thus making of the future a Moloch to which the real man is sacrificed in favor of a man who is not real but is always still to come."[29]

Unquestionably, this decision-making process is a difficult enterprise; it is nevertheless certain that whenever Christians involve themselves in a movement against injustice, they do so not in order to lay claim to a dignity that is undeserved, but to proclaim a dignity that has for too long gone unrecognized and unheeded. The rebellion, in other words, takes place not in order that we shall be, but because we are. Moreover, as Rosemary Ruether notes, precisely when "the 'we shall be' grows so domineering as to cancel out the 'we are' and becomes a rationale for oppression and murder, then the rebel has lost the basis of his original rebellion and has no alternative but to die himself."[30]

Our analysis of the ethics of hope suggests that it employs a methodology of juxtaposition in which an attempt is made, not only to explain and interpret the past, but also to correlate the various elements of present experience without, at the same time, closing the door to the future.[31] Along with situational ethics, an ethics of hope regards the present as real and as having an element of independence, but in the name of memory and for the sake of human imagination, the temptation to apotheosize the present is resisted. In light of present experience the past is challenged, but the present is called to task by the memory of the past, and the claims of both the present and the past are relativized insofar as Christians think and live in light of a future of hope.

133

If we take seriously the fact that the faith-commitment of Christianity is truly historical, as well as fully incarnational and essentially eschatological, we can then close our eyes to the past, present, or future only at the cost of sacrificing an authentic and adequate ethical methodology. And yet it is inevitable that our historical memory, our hope for the future, and our present experience should at times challenge and even contradict one another, because there is an undeniable element of discontinuity in the history of humanity's relationship to God; this cannot help but have an effect upon human efforts to comprehend in an ethically significant way the compass and progress of our personal and social history. How we react to this discontinuity, however, will determine the structure of our ethical reflection. It makes a difference, in other words, whether decisive emphasis is given to the past, to the present, or finally to the future.

My own inclination, on the basis both of the more recent systematic understanding of eschatology by men like Teilhard, Moltmann, and other theologians of hope, and of an existential-phenomenological analysis of humanity as an historically dynamic reality, is to put the emphasis on the future. Then, of course, the next question centers on the nature of the future, that is, whether it is a truly new and open future with elements of the unexpected, or whether it is closed and predetermined; in other terms, the question is whether Christians must interpret history as basically eschatological or as teleological. Here the evidence of the Christian tradition points to an eschatological interpretation of the future that posits a creative discontinuity between it and the past and present. Christian messianism did not in fact fulfill Israel's expectations as these were originally formulated. On the contrary, these expectations were disappointed, but in the process the meaning of Israel's own existence was broadened and deepened by a new hope.

Thus it is part of the meaning of eschatology to shake reality out of its established categories; insofar as the Christian experience makes sense only from within the perspective of eschatology, it is not unreasonable to expect that the task of theology, and hence of Christian ethics, is not merely to reconcile faith to experience, but also to introduce an element of creative conflict which has the effect of transforming finally the processes of secular and human history. As Harvey Cox has said, "merely to reconcile theology to existing reality is to forget the crucial eschatological factor, the one that reminds us that existing reality is provisional, is part of 'this passing age,' and therefore cannot be taken with ultimate seriousness."[32] Only by allowing for, demanding, and even effecting, creative transformation in the light of eschatology does an ethics of hope truly acknowledge the legitimate criticism of Marx against religion, that finally interpretation of the world must bear fruit in a changing of the world and in a recognition of the value of human labors.

What enables us as believers to engage in this creative transformation is a kind of "forward memory" which prods us to the work of the present moment. In relation to the eschatological promises, Christians may be said to face the task of remembering the future; yet precisely to the extent that the future remains uncompleted, our activity as Christians is one not only of anticipation and expectation but also of creative involvement. Thus both the past and the future impinge upon the shaping of the present. In remembering the past and creatively anticipating the future, Christians are empowered to work the supreme miracle of assisting others, especially those oppressed, to the realization that their deepest aspirations really are not fantasies.[33]

The interplay of past, present, and future, works itself out in the vital relationships that operate among faith, charity and hope. Although the appearance of faith lies rooted deep within our common past as Christians, its efficacy is uncurtailed, for the character of faith reveals its true countenance only in the attitude of hope for the future, and in the activity of love in the present. Without fear of distorting the reality of faith, we may say that Christian love is faith that is inspired to action in the present, while hope is that freedom to plan and to act which arises from a faith that is oriented toward the future. Jesus Christ frees Christians to faith, faith frees them to hope, and hope frees them to love in a way that transforms the earth. Without exaggeration, then, it may be said that our best reason for hoping, is that God needs us on the earth and, more importantly, he needs us because he first loves us.

For Christian living, faith is the authority, love is its reason and motive, and hope is its dynamism. The same may be said of Christian ethics. In the effort to embody the spirit of Christianity, there is always the need for ascetic discipline and even for a "flight from the world." But this flight is always what Metz has called a "**Flucht nach vorn**;" this is never a flight out of the world, but rather a flight forward with the world into the future in which Christians need not fear solidarity with the world, but only conformity to it.[34] It is for the sake of the future that action is undertaken, but it is for the very same reason that some activity is foregone, that pain is undergone, and that suffering is endured. But if it is true that for Christians not everything is allowed, so it is also true that not everything is to be endured. It is certain, however, that in moving into the future through determining the ethical course of action, Christians must be inspired by faith, motivated by love, and freed and directed by hope.

A Summation

In a sense this study has been a commentary on the observation of Helmut Thielicke that if Christian ethics is not eschatological, it is nothing.[35] I wish now only to suggest that the basic insight contained in this idea centers on the necessary relationship between a faith-commitment and the realization of authentic theologizing. It seems naive and commonplace to repeat that Christian theology must develop within a context of faith, and that within this same context, and on the theological foundations it provides, the task of Christian ethics must be initiated and pursued. And yet too much of Christian ethics, at least as it has come down to us through the manuals of Roman Catholicism, has given the impression that correct ethical decisions, instead of arising out of a faith-commitment, are rather the beginnings of, and means of attaining, a certain asceticism and spirituality. Unintentionally, no doubt, but still, understandably, the tradition of Catholic moralism in this way opened itself to the charge of "works-salvationism." The place or need of faith was not denied, but the implications and effects of living the faith-life were not adequately regarded in exploring and explaining the process of moral decision-making.

In effect, what seems to have happened is that the ancient ideal of Anselm and Augustine, that of "fides quaerens intellectum," was not taken seriously in the often difficult task of uncovering the appropriate course of action to be undertaken given one's concrete situation. The reality of "charism" ceased to have any bearing in the process of ethical evaluations and determinations. The place for a "discernment of spirits" was similarly slighted, all of which indicates that a dichotomy was made between Christian ethics, on the one hand, and asceticism and spirituality, on the other. Such a divorce between ethics and asceticism is detrimental to, and distortive of, these two realities themselves and our understanding of them.

Here, however, I am concerned to point out only how ethics can be aided by the asceticism of faith. The argument is developed in some such fashion as this. The Christian faith-response is a totally personal one, involving the integrated intellectual, volitional, and affective resources of the individual. Precisely because of its deeply-rooted personal character involving the individual in a relationship with Christ, faith may be said to belong more to the order of being, than of having. A fundamental orientation of a person toward the revelation of God through Christ and his Church is established, with the result that the individual is marked by a sensitivity toward, and appreciation of, the workings and expectations of God.

Faith in God, or life in the Spirit of God, is at the same time an openness also to the offer of the gifts of the Spirit, gifts which serve both to increase the believer's sense of obligation and responsibility, and to facilitate his or her perception of the most appropriate ethical response to the situation presenting itself. Thus, to the extent that situations are contingent and singular, to that same extent does the need for charism and for the art of discernment become more apparent in the effort to deal with every situation most responsibly.[36]

But this is only one side of the story. The other side has to do with the fact that moral values exist not in isolation, but in basic continuity with human and cultural values, to the point even that moral values are embodied in intellectual, emotional, and social values. Christian ethics must struggle, then, to impress the viewpoint of faith, the dynamism of hope, the work of charity, and the power of grace, upon the human and cultural dimensions of life so as to elicit the full meaning of these values and thus allow them even greater realization.[37]

Any authentic Christian ethic must necessarily embrace the physical, social, and cosmic dimensions of human expectations. This calls for a serious investigation into the resources of human and physical energy, and for a realistic appraisal of the best means for their development. Human reason, then, is never relieved of its task of making the most of reality's potential, and yet, at the same time, when reason is amplified, enriched, and enlightened by faith, and thus becomes a faithful reason, sparks begin to fly. Horizons are extended, new worlds come into focus and, most of all, people begin to hope, now no longer simply for a better "life out of life," but for a "life out of death." Hope is the glow of faith and the fire of love in this in-between time; it is the dynamism which allows, liberates and encourages faith to be active in love, even when reason can see no reason except to despair, to be cynical, and to hate.

The significance of ethical reflections which are shaped by a theology of promise-inspired hope lies in their success in avoiding the naturalistic reductionism of liberal theology's evolutionary progress without, however, undermining our legitimate and necessary sense of human responsibility and accountability for our personal and social history, and for the physical preservation and development of the world. In our hope for the appearance of the new future, we know as Christians that our efforts in history are always subject to the divine judgment of completion and final transformation; at the same time, we believe that our achievements for righteousness and justice are recognizable and shall endure. Finally, the pain of present injustices, the frustrations arising from obstacles encountered in the movement toward the coming future of God, the certainty of a death still to come, all serve to remind us that for now the power of the resurrection is ours to enjoy only under the shadow of Christ's cross, which guarantees that both the past and the present shall be transformed in the future of the new creation, the **novum ultimum**. And yet the promises of God imply a covenantal relationship which leaves no doubt in our minds as to God's expectation of, and need for, our co-operation with him in history.

As Schillebeeckx has suggested, here lies the paradox of Christianity: "We tread in the footsteps of the God who is to come to us from the future and, in so doing, it is still we who make history."[38] In an attitude of expectant creativity, which is expressed in our confident responsibility, we live as believers in active commitment to the future of the world, while all the time recognizing and proclaiming God's initiative in inaugurating a new future which we, by ourselves, do not merit in any strict sense, but which we must actively dispose ourselves for. This is to say, that it is in and through hope that we have been liberated to the freedom to work for, and to receive, what God has promised us.

We are free to be and to do what we are called to be and to do. But this very description of the human situation indicates at once that we are not autonomous and self-sufficient. Our freedom is dialogical, worked out in responsive obedience to a divine summons that appears under the form of a promise which is at once supportive in its exhortations and directive in its demands. At long last freedom is not defined in negative terms of separation, division, and isolation (freedom from), but rather, as both Teilhard and Moltmann have indicated, in positive terms of reconciliation, unity, peace, justice, and community (freedom for). For without a doubt, God's hope for us, and our hope for ourselves and for others, is that all may be one in God in the fullness of time.

As Christians we are coming alive to our social responsibilities, and in this enterprise, just as we dare not buy law and order at the price of justice, so neither may we laud the efficacy of any proposed means as the sole and final criterion in resisting injustice and working for its removal. For Christians, the eschatological promises establish the boundaries for ethical decisions, and in light of these promises we must question and decide about the appropriate forms of revolutionary involvement. Both Marxists and Christians attempt to deal with given social, economic and political circumstances in light of a future which will bring a negation of these circumstances. But there are obvious differences in perspective.

For Marxists, the new future is the product solely of historical processes, while for Christians, the historical process is the framework within which they labor in preparing the foundations of the new future that retains always an element of gratuity. Whereas Marxists contend that the content of the future is determined by man, Christians look to a future which is determined by God, who nevertheless constantly calls us to participation in the labor of building the coming kingdom. Marxist thinking, then, moves more in the direction of political humanism, while the messianic humanism of Christianity allows for and expects a less fanatically independent involvement in the world.

For all its idealism, Christianity remembers that the ideal is realized only as gift. This element of gratuity or grace allows for the possibility of joy which remains curtailed by the Pelagian character of political humanism. Moreover, because the future's transcendence already is experienced by believers as a deeply transforming power in the present and thus serves as a point of critical reference, there need be no commitment to cross-purposes in Christians' hope-filled existence in light of the promised future and their present socio-political awareness and involvement. Rather, with a vision intensified and maintained by faith and hope in a new future, Christians confront the inadequacies of the present in a spirit of love. Still, some tension does remain between present commitment and future expectation, between living and acting under the promise and awaiting its fulfillment.

It must be admitted that the distinction between political human-ism and messianic humanism presupposes a degree of openness on the part of the believer, such that evidence is received and accepted concerning the very existence of any transcendent future. Only after the initial acceptance of the transcendent do the subsequent questions arise concerning the relationship and reciprocal influences between this transcendent and ourselves. Only then must we decide to stress either continuity or discontinuity. Thus, there must first be a gospel accepted as such, before we may admit to either its possible encour-agements for, or limitations upon, human activity; only in the context of faith do we begin to suspect the full possibilities of pregnant absence. We can hope in joy only if we believe, because only in the context of faith does our contingency appear, not as a cause for despair and desperate measures, but as a promise and condi-tion for fulfillment with the inauguration of the new future, the revolution to end all revolutions.

As an attempt to explain Christianity's eschatological hope with its implications for personal and social existence, an ethics of hope indicates that we are saved neither by faith alone nor by works alone. What is called for is faith that is expressed in love (Gal. 5:6), a kind of expectant creativity and involved transcendence leading to a commitment without fanaticism and destruction, a commit-ment in which hatred has no place even if disciplined violence sometimes does. In moving toward a new future which is seen as the common inheritance of all people, hope must serve as the center and source of creativity within the ethics of a "faith active in love," an ethics which often enough in the past has been too comfortable with arrangements of the status quo and has taken pride in its sensitivity to human suffering, while remaining satisfied with the temporary alleviation of afflictions instead of uncovering and challenging the very cause of these afflictions.[39] Whereas the ethics of faith active in love may be reluctant or unable to recognize such realities as "power structures" and "established oppressions" in the areas of politics, economics and race relations, an ethics of hope in the future is an integral part of a political theology which lives with the possibility—not to say the expectation—that power must be seized in the movements to overcome socially-sanctioned oppressions on whatever level. Reconciliation always demands and involves personal and social transformations.

The ethical dimension of any religion which serves as the opiate of the people appears in the planning and implementation of social programs that offer charity without justice. Such programs are designed with the intention, it seems, of dulling the sufferers' awareness of pain without, however, lancing the source of infection and, thereby, opening the way to any real healing. In effect, such programs encourage the oppressed to be satisfied with, and grateful for, the loss or diminution of pain, even though they continue to be knowingly and freely deprived by society both of the available means of true recovery and of any hope for further growth. A theology of hope has it within its power to reveal both this enervating form of religion and this ethics of faith without effective action, and of charity without justice, for what they are—deviate forms of Christianity. The reality of a future which makes its presence felt every day through promise and in hope inspires an ethics that labors for the creation of a situation in which the fullness of humanity can be anticipated; at the same time, moreover, an ethics of hope realizes that every step forward toward the future takes place in the here and now; thus we have the foundations for a concrete and effective involvement in the present. Demands that are both real and realistic are here made upon Christians who always expect to be, and anticipate being, all that they have the capacity to be in themselves and through the grace of God.

It may be fairly stated, then, that an adequate Christian ethics is one finally which not only arises from our hope and trust in the total lordship of Christ, but also has the effect of stirring up in us and in others "live hopes that are braced for action and prepared to suffer, hopes of the kingdom of God that is coming to earth in order to transform it."[40] An ethics of Christian hope strives, in other words, to continue and expand the proleptic realization of the divine lordship which was dramatically signalled in the resurrection of Christ. Through the influence of such an ethics, and under its auspices, all people are invited and encouraged to the obedience of faith by means of which they may dispose themselves for receiving the fullness of eschatological freedom and human dignity.

In this way hope embodies itself in an ethics which is one with Christianity's mission, namely, the continuing facilitation of humanity's reconciliation with God and his future. Now, however, the saving action of God comes to be represented, not merely in the notions of "salvation of the soul, individual rescue from the world, comfort for the troubled conscience," but more in the realities of "the eschatological **hope of justice**, the **humanizing** of man, the **socializing** of humanity, **peace** for all creation." Moreover, in keeping with its mission of challenging the existing situation and of seeking for new opportunities of bringing history "into ever better correspondence to the promised future," an ethics of hope may be rightly regarded as an effort at the "historic transformation of life," which alters the human conditions of possibility so that what now seems impossible becomes possible.[41]

At least on this level, then, an ethics of Christian hope goes a long way toward meeting the challenge offered by the Marxist philosopher, Roger Garaudy, when he said that we are faced with "the duty of seeing to it that every man becomes a man, a flaming hearth of initiative, a poet in the deepest sense of the word; one who has experienced, day by day, the creative surpassing of himself— what Christians call his transcendence and we [Marxists] call his authentic humanity." Christians and Marxists can unite in a "mutual willingness to stretch man's creative energies to the maximum for the sake of realizing a total man."[42] In recognition of the human need and capacity to create, an ethics of Christian hope is convinced that human beings prepare themselves to go beyond the world by going through it, that they are conditioned to transcend it by traversing it. Thus Christians make a mockery of their heritage and fools of themselves if they presume to gain a new future with empty heads, idle hands, and eyes blind to the world around them. Rather, the ascent to God follows the path of transforming and constructing the earth with more lucidity of mind, more intensity of action, and more vehemency of passion.[43]

In the final analysis, both Christians and Marxists will be judged in light of their struggle to remake the world and thereby to calm humanity's outrage of conscience. For Christians, however, human involvement in history is seen always as dynamically related to God's eschatological promises. I suggest, therefore, in line with Teilhard's views, that our efforts at human and divine reconciliation are true and necessary foundations of God's kingdom, so that by God's graciousness we fulfill under his guiding assistance the role of co-creators with him of his kingdom. What we achieve in history receives the touch of God's final transfiguration and is thereby transformed into the enduring successes of his new future.

In conclusion, then, our exploration into the character of Christian hope leads us to suggest that as a formal dynamism in the task of ethical reflection, hope serves both as a constructive and liberating impulse and as a guiding and directing force. Under hope's influence Christians are reminded of the work of God and of his promise in Jesus Christ, who stands in the history of humanity as the incarnation of God's gospel and command. Speaking figuratively, the reality of hope operates in the lives of Christians like a brave and careful advance scout, who dashes on ahead of the pilgrim people to look into the promised land of the future, but who must always return to spur the people on and to show them the way. Christian hope, then, is doubly gifted: it embraces both the vision of what is positive in the desirable future and a knowledge of those negative forces in the present, which pose a threat to the forward movement toward God's promised future.[44]

Thus, as God's people moving toward the advancing kingdom, our hope informs us of several things. We know, first of all, that the way to the future is indeed open, that there is, in fact, a future for us to enjoy, and that this future is a true future, whose newness is neither a repetition of past glories, nor a dream of idealistic projections from past and present possibilities. Moreover, although our new future now exists fully only in promise and in our hopeful anticipation of it, both the broad horizons of the future's boundaries and the general contours of the pathway leading to its borders already draw their reality from the very terms of the promise, especially as these have been incarnated in the life and teaching of Jesus. Finally, insofar as hope knows that the promise of the new future is real, it infuses us with the desire and willingness, but also the need, to labor creatively for the realization of that future's arrival in and through the final act of God's transformation of our efforts. At the same time, because hope sees that the new future is not totally amorphous, it lends a definite shape to our labors in our movement through time, such that we cannot approach the future of God in precision from, or contradiction to, the directive and compelling words of the divine promise.

In effect, then, by preparing and building up the earth for the future's approach, we move at the same time closer to the new future of God through our efforts to anticipate its arrival by shaping the present in accordance with the vision of promised fulfillment. Insofar as we are to prepare for and anticipate the new future of God's kingdom in all things, we will fulfill our mission, sometimes through the works of active creation under the attraction of the gospel, sometimes through the pains of active suffering that are associated with the guidelines set forth in the divine commands. It is in the historical effort to determine in hope whether such active creation or active endurance is demanded and expected that the shape of Christian ethics evolves.

Here the requirements of present love are operative. Thus, in a theological ethics which is rooted in faith-remembered promises, hope is the compass which gives expression to our desire to be some-where other than where we presently are; it is also the instrument upon which we rely in order to assure ourselves that we are not drifting from the direction leading to the promised land of the future. But all the while, love is the rudder which must be manned in the daily effort to ensure that neither the winds of self-deception and human pride, nor the currents of greed and fear, distract us from the vision we harbor, or deter us from the struggle to reach at last our promised goal.

For us as Christians, one thing, at least, is certain: the meaning of our lives is unavoidably eschatological. It follows that our ethics must be shaped accordingly. Precisely insofar as our ethics indicates the way to the promised kingdom of God, the way to sharing in the future God desires for us, it is an eschatological ethics, that is, one by means of which, in the light of God's promise and with the vision, freedom and strength it provides, we are guided and aided in our efforts to prepare the way of the Lord. Our activity is always enlivened and directed by the coming kingdom under whose sign we live, and whose witnesses and prophets we must be. Living ethically means for us as Christians that we are engaged in an escha-tological practice; we do the future ahead of time in the present. We labor in hope and in love in order to change the world "in the expectation of the divine change."[45]

Our attitude, then, cannot be one either of allowing no change or of allowing any and all changes, of initiating nothing or of initiating everything. We do not leave everything to God, nor do we leave nothing to him. We have shared dominion and responsibility with

144

God, and we must carefully and conscientiously investigate the extent of this sharing in order to learn the precise shape of our responsibility. Whatever other forms our investigation may take, it must also include our engagement with God in prayer, for only from within a life of prayer can we be fully informed and our consciences properly formed.

CHAPTER V

REFERENCES

1. David L. Fleming, S.J., "Passion" in the Spiritual Writings of Teilhard de Chardin: A Study of Detachment and Diminishment, A Doctoral Dissertation presented to The Catholic University of America, 1969 (Ann Arbor, Michigan: University Microfilms, 1970), pp. 6-9.

2. Pierre Teilhard de Chardin, The Divine Milieu (New York: Harper Torchbooks, 1965), p. 152; also confer Romeo Walter Brooks, The Influence of the Spirituality of Teilhard de Chardin on Religious Life, A Doctoral Dissertation presented to Marquette University, 1971 (Ann Arbor, Michigan: University Microfilms, 1971), pp. 217-18.

3. These ideas appear in Teilhard's letters to Blondel which are collected in Pierre Teilhard de Chardin—Maurice Blondel Correspondence, with Notes and Commentary by Henri de Lubac, S.J., trans. William Whitman (New York: Herder & Herder, 1967), p. 33.

4. Brooks, Influence of the Spirituality of Teilhard, p. 241.

5. Jürgen Moltmann, Theology of Hope, trans. James W. Leitch (New York: Harper & Row, 1967), pp. 86, 88.

6. Ibid., pp. 285, 287.

7. Ibid., p. 326.

8. See Donald P. Gray in his response to Wolfhart Pannenberg, "Future and Unity," Hope and the Future of Man, ed. Ewert H. Cousins (Phila.: Fortress Press, 1972), p. 82.

9. Teilhard, Teilhard—Blondel Correspondence, p. 34.

10. This dialectical tension in hope is developed in Philip Hefner, "The Future as Our Future: A Teilhardian Perspective," Hope and the Future of Man, pp. 15-39 at 35-6.

11. Hope's implication of temporal involvement is developed in Johannes B. Metz, "Creative Hope," New Theology No. 5, eds. Martin Marty and Dean Peerman (New York: Macmillan, 1968), pp. 130-41 at 134, 138.

12. See Henri de Lubac, S.J., The Religion of Teilhard de Chardin, trans. René Hague (New York: Image Books, 1968), p. 216.

13. Reinhold Niebuhr, Does Civilization Need Religion? (New York: The Macmillan Company, 1927), p. 12.

14. For a discussion of the balances and characteristics of Christian hope see Martin E. Marty, The Search for a Usable Future (New York: Harper & Row, 1969), p. 86, and Gerald G. O'Collins, S.J., Man and His New Hopes (New York: Herder & Herder, 1969), pp. 91-6. See also Dietrich Bonhoeffer, Letters and Papers from Prison, ed. Eberhard Bethge, trans. Reginald H. Fuller (New York: Macmillan Paperbacks, 1962), pp. 165-66, 208-9, 204-6. Interesting observations are made in Eric Mascall, "The Scientific Outlook and the Christian Message," The Evolving World and Theology, Concilium Series, vol. 26, ed. Johannes B. Metz (New York: Paulist Press, 1967), pp. 125-33 at 132. Mascall insists here that the Christian doctrine of the resurrection of the body has implications which should expose as aberrant any theoretical or practical movement that would deny or ridicule a serious concern for the welfare of material creation. Because of the fact that by our physical or bodily constitution we are quite literally a part of the material world, the doctrine of personal resurrection "entails nothing less than the ultimate transfiguration of the material world and its absorption into Christ." Thus, when directed toward Christianity, the Marxist critique of religion, especially as an opiate of the people, can only be explained as a misunderstanding on the part of Marxist theorists, or as a legitimate criticism of Christianity's unchristian teachings arising from, and expressing, a Manichaean spirituality which portrays human beatitude as consisting ideally "in a complete break with the realm of matter and a definite escape from bodily existence."

15. Emmanuel Mesthene, "Religious Values in the Age of Technology," The Evolving World and Theology, pp. 109-24 at 122.

16. Juan Alfaro, "Christian Hope and the Hopes of Mankind," Dimensions of Spirituality, Concilium Series, Vol. 59, ed. Christian Duquoc (New York: Herder & Herder, 1970), pp. 59-69 at 68-9.

17. Jürgen Moltmann, Religion, Revolution, and the Future, trans. M. Douglas Meeks (New York: Charles Scribner's Sons, 1969), pp. 6, 16.

18. Christopher F. Mooney, S.J., The Making of Man: Essays in the Christian Spirit (New York: Paulist Press, 1971), pp. 58-9.

19. The notion of "contrast-experience" is taken from Edward Schillebeeckx, O.P., God The Future of Man, trans. N. D. Smith (New York: Sheed & Ward, 1968), pp. 153-54, 159.

20. Ibid., p. 197.

21. Ibid., p. 195.

22. Josef Pieper, Hope and History, trans. Richard and Clara Winston (New York: Herder & Herder, 1969), p. 91.

23. Piet Fransen, S.J., "Hope and Anthropology: Is There Still Prophecy in the Church?," The God Experience: Essays in Hope, ed. Joseph P. Whelan, S.J. (New York, Newman Press, 1971), pp. 138-67 at 167.

24. Jürgen Moltmann, "Antwort auf die Kritik der Theologie der Hoffnung," Diskussion über die "Theologie der Hoffnung," ed. Wolf-Dieter Marsch (München: Chr. Kaiser Verlag, 1967), p. 209.

25. Carl E. Braaten, The Future of God: The Revolutionary Dynamics of Hope (New York: Harper & Row, 1969), p. 46.

26. Ibid., p. 48.

27. O'Collins, Man and His Hopes, p. 127.

28. Patrick Kerans, S.J., "Hope, Objectivity, and Technical Culture," Continuum, 7, no. 4 (Winter, 1970), pp. 570-82 at 573.

29. Roger Garaudy, From Anathema to Dialogue, trans. Luke O'Neill (New York: Herder & Herder, 1966) p. 60.

30. Rosemary Ruether, The Radical Kingdom: The Western Experience of Messianic Hope (New York: Harper & Row, 1970), p. 143. See also pages 133-43 where Ruether employs an analysis of rebellion developed by Albert Camus in Man in Revolt (1951).

31. For the idea of a methodology of juxtaposition I am indebted to Harvey Cox, The Feast of Fools: A Theological Essay on Festivity and Fantasy (Cambridge, Mass.: Harvard University Press, 1969), pp. 131-38.

32. Ibid., p. 135. Similar expressions of the role of eschatology in Christian Ethics are found in Amos N. Wilder, Eschatology and Ethics in the Teaching of Jesus (New York: Harper & Brothers, rev. ed., 1950), p. 36: ". . . the essential inspiration of . . . eschatology remains what it was with Jesus, what it was in Jewish eschatology at its best: the appeal of the ethical consciousness against things as they are, and the incontrovertible assurance of faith that God will act." See also Wolfhart Pannenberg, Theology and the Kingdom of God (Phila.: Westminster Press, 1969), pp. 105-06 where the author argues that ". . . within the present human reality ethics must discover the tendencies toward the possible amelioration of present life. Honestly confronting what is, ethics must point to what is to be, what can be, what ought to be." Finally see Vernard Eller, The Promise: Ethics in the Kingdom of God (Garden City, New York: Doubleday, 1970), p. 208: "The aim of morality is not to make human existence tolerable under conditions of the present but to help move it toward its destiny. Its aim is not to make a man comfortable in regard to what he is but to challenge him to become what he can be and what God is offering to make of him."

33. The idea of "forward memory" is taken from E. Mark Stern and Bert G. Marino, Psychotheology, (Paramus, N.J.: Newman Press, 1970), p. 95.

34. Johannes B. Metz, Theology of the World, trans. William Glen-Doepel (New York: Herder & Herder, 1969), p. 102; also see the German edition, Zur Theologie der Welt (Mainz: Matthias Grünewald Verlag, 1968), p. 93.

149

35. Helmut Thielicke, Theological Ethics, ed. William H. Lazareth, Vol. 1: Foundations (Phila.: Fortress Press, 1966), p. 47.

36. See Robert H. Springer, S.J., "Conscience, Behavioral Science, and Absolutes," Absolutes in Moral Theology?, ed. Charles E. Curran (Washington: Corpus Books, 1968), pp. 19-56 at 25-7.

37. Philippe Delhaye, "The Contribution of Vatican II to Moral Theology," Man in a New Society, Concilium Series, Vol. 75, ed. Franz Böckle (New York: Herder & Herder, 1972), pp. 58-67 at 67.

38. Schillebeeckx, God the Future of Man, p. 190.

39. On this point see Carl E. Braaten, "Toward a Theology of Hope," New Theology No. 5, pp. 90-111 at 107.

40. Moltmann, Theology of Hope, p. 328.

41. Ibid., pp. 329-30.

42. Garaudy, From Anathema to Dialogue, pp. 123, 120.

43. Roger Garaudy, "Communists and Christians in Dialogue," New Theology No. 5, pp. 212-21 at 220-21.

44. The basic simile regarding the function of hope was suggested by Carl E. Braaten, "The Significance of the Future: An Eschatological Perspective," Hope and the Future of Man, pp. 40-54 at 44.

45. The ideas here are derived largely from Carl E. Braaten, Eschatology and Ethics. Essays on the Theology and Ethics of the Kingdom of God (Minneapolis: Augsburg Publishing House, 1974). See especially Ch. 7, "Eschatology: The Key to Christian Ethics," pp. 105-122. Also see Moltmann, Theology of Hope, p. 84.

WORKS CITED

Abbott, Walter M., S.J. ed. The Documents of Vatican II, trans. ed. Joseph Gallagher. New York: The America Press, 1966.

Alfaro, Juan. "Christian Hope and the Hopes of Mankind." Dimensions of Spirituality, Concilium Series, Vol. 59, ed. Christian Duquoc. New York: Herder and Herder, 1970, pp. 59-69.

Alves, Rubem A. A Theology of Human Hope. Washington: Corpus Books, 1969.

_____. "Some Thoughts on a Program for Ethics." Union Seminary Quarterly Review, XXVI, No. 2 (Winter, 1971), 153-70.

Arsenault, Fernand. "L'Ethique social chez Teilhard de Chardin." Sciences Religieuses/Studies in Religion 1, No. 1 (1971), 25-44.

Braaten, Carl E. "American Historical Experience and Christian Reflection." Projections: Shaping an American Theology for the Future, eds. Thomas F. O'Meara and Donald M. Weisser. Garden City, New York: Doubleday Image Books, 1970, pp. 93-115.

_____. Eschatology and Ethics. Essays on the Theology and Ethics of the Kingdom of God. Minneapolis: Augsburg Publishing House, 1974.

_____. The Future of God. The Revolutionary Dynamics of Hope. New York: Harper and Row, 1969.

_____. "The Significance of the Future: An Eschatological Perspective." Hope and the Future of Man, ed. Ewert H. Cousins. Phila.: Fortress Press, 1972, pp. 40-54.

_____. "Toward a Theology of Hope." New Theology No. 5 eds. Martin Marty and Dean Peerman. New York: Macmillan, 1968, pp. 90-111.

Brooks, Romeo Walter. The Influence of the Spirituality of Teilhard de Chardin on Religious Life. A Doctoral Dissertation Presented to Marquette University, 1971. Ann Arbor, Mich.: University Microfilms, 1971.

Burney, Pierre. "Sketch for a Morality of Love: A Tentative Application of Teilhardian Methods." The Teilhard Review, 4 (Winter, 1969-70), 60-71.

Capps, Walter H. "An Assessment of the Theological Side of the School of Hope," Cross Currents, XVIII, No. 3 (Summer, 1968), 319-35.

_____. Time Invades the Cathedral. Tensions in the School of Hope. Phila.: Fortress Press, 1972.

Cassirer, Ernst. An Essay on Man. Garden City, N.Y.: Doubleday, 1953.

Cox, Harvey. On Not Leaving It To The Snake. New York: Macmillan Paperbacks, 1969.

_____. The Feast of Fools. A Theological Essay on Festivity and Fantasy. Cambridge, Mass.: Harvard Univ. Press, 1969.

Delhaye, Philippe. "The Contribution of Vatican II to Moral Theology." Man in a New Society, Concilium Series, Vol. 75, ed. Franz Böckle. New York: Herder and Herder, 1972, pp. 58-67.

de Lubac, Henri, S.J. Teilhard de Chardin: The Man and His Meaning, trans. René Hague, New York: Hawthorn Books, 1965.

_____. The Religion of Teilhard de Chardin, trans. René Hague. New York: Image Books, 1968.

Devaux, Andre-A. "Teilhard et la construction d'une morale pour notre temps." Revue Teilhard de Chardin, 6, No. 23 (1965), 31-8.

Dulles, Avery, S.J. "An Apologetics of Hope." The God Experience. Essays in Hope, ed. Joseph P. Whelan, S.J. New York: Newman Press, 1971, pp. 244-63.

Dupré, Louis. "Hope and Transcendence." The God Experience. Essays in Hope, ed. Joseph P. Whelan, S.J. New York: Newman Press, 1971, pp. 217-25.

_____. "The Existentialist Connections of Situation Ethics." The Future of Ethics and Moral Theology, eds. Don Brezine and James V. McGlynn. Chicago: Argus Communications, 1968, pp. 106-13.

Eller, Vernard. "Comments on An Unsolicited Series." The Christian Century, 85, No. 15 (April 10, 1968), 459-60.

_____. The Promise: Ethics in the Kingdom of God. Garden City, N.Y.: Doubleday, 1970.

Faricy, Robert L., S.J. Teilhard de Chardin's Theology of the Christian in the World. New York: Sheed and Ward, 1967.

Fleming, David L., S.J. "Passion" in the Spiritual Writings of Teilhard de Chardin: A Study of Detachment and Diminishment. A Doctoral Dissertation Presented to The Catholic University of America. Ann Arbor, Mich.: University Microfilms, 1970.

Fransen, Piet, S.J. "Hope and Anthropology: Is There Still Prophecy in the Church?" The God Experience. Essays in Hope, ed. Joseph P. Whelan, S.J. New York: Newman Press, 1971, pp. 138-67.

Fromm, Erich. The Revolution of Hope. Toward a Humanized Technology. New York: Bantam Books, 1968.

Garaudy, Roger. "Communists and Christians in Dialogue." New Theology No. 5, eds. Martin Marty and Dean Peerman. New York: Macmillan, 1968, pp. 212-21.

_____. From Anathema to Dialogue, trans. Luke O'Neill. New York: Herder and Herder, 1966.

Gray, Donald P. "Future and Unity." Hope and the Future of Man, ed. Ewert H. Cousins. Phila.: Fortress Press, 1972.

_____. "Teilhard's Vision of Love." Dimensions of the Future. The Spirituality of Teilhard de Chardin, eds. Marvin Kessler and Bernard Brown. Washington: Corpus Books, 1968, pp. 73-98.

Hefner, Philip. "The Future as Our Future: A Teilhardian Perspective." Hope and the Future of Man, ed. Ewert H. Cousins. Phila.: Fortress Press, 1972. pp. 15-39.

Hermann, Ingo. The Experience of Faith, trans. Daniel Coogan. New York: Kenedy and Sons, 1966.

Hunsinger, George. "The Crucified God and the Political Theology of Violence: A Critical Survey of Jürgen Moltmann's Recent Thought: I and II," The Heythrop Journal, XIV, No. 3 and 4 (July and October, 1973), 266-79; 379-95.

Kerans, Patrick, S.J. "Hope, Objectivity, and Technical Culture." Continuum, 7, No. 4 (Winter, 1970), 570-82.

Lynch, William F., S.J. "Images of Faith," Continuum, 7 (1969-70), 187-94.

_____. Images of Hope: Imagination as Healer of the Hopeless. New York: Mentor-Omega Books, 1966.

Macquarrie, John. Three Issues in Ethics. New York: Harper and Row, 1970.

Marcel, Gabriel. Homo Viator: Introduction to a Metaphysics of Hope, trans. Emma Craufurd. New York: Harper Torchbooks, 1962.

_____. The Mystery of Being. Vol. II. Faith and Reality, trans. René Hague. Chicago: Henry Regnery Co., Gateway Ed., 1960.

Marcuse, Robert. Eros and Civilization. Boston: Beacon Press, 1955.

_____. One Dimensional Man. Boston: Beacon Press, 1966.

Marty, Martin E. The Search for a Usable Future. New York: Harper and Row, 1969.

McCabe, Herbert. What Is Ethics All About? A Re-evaluation of Law, Love, and Language. Washington: Corpus Books, 1969.

Mesthene, Emmanuel. "Religious Values in The Age of Technology." The Evolving World and Theology, Concilium Series, Vol. 26, ed. Johannes B. Metz. New York: Paulist Press, 1967, pp. 109-24.

Metz, Johannes B. "Creative Hope." New Theology No. 5, eds. Martin Marty and Dean Peerman. New York: Macmillan, 1968, pp. 130-41.

_____. Theology of the World, trans. William Glen-Doepel. New York: Herder and Herder, 1969.

_____. Zur Theologie der Welt. Mainz: Matthias Grünewald Verlag, 1968.

Migliore, Daniel L. "Biblical Eschatology and Political Hermeneutics." Theology Today, XXVI (1969), 116-32.

Moltmann, Jürgen, "Antwort auf die Kritik der Theologie der Hoffnung." Diskussion über die "Theologie der Hoffnung," ed. Wolf-Dieter Marsch. München: Chr. Kaiser Verlag, 1967.

_____. Hope and Planning, trans. Margaret Clarkson. New York: Harper and Row, 1971.

_____. "Hope without Faith: An Eschatological Humanism without God." Is God Dead?, Concilium Series, Vol. 16, ed. Johannes B. Metz. New York: Paulist Press, 1964, pp. 25-40.

_____. Religion, Revolution, and The Future, trans. M. Douglas Meeks. New York: Charles Scribner's Sons, 1969.

_____. The Church in the Power of the Spirit. A Contribution to Messianic Ecclesiology, trans. Margaret Kohl. New York: Harper and Row, 1977.

_____. The Crucified God. The Cross of Christ as the Foundation and Criticism of Christian Theology, trans. R. A. Wilson and John Bowden. New York: Harper and Row, 1974.

155

_____. The Experiment Hope, ed., trans., with foreword by M. Douglas Meeks. Phila.: Fortress Press, 1975.

_____. "Theology as Eschatology." The Future of Hope. Theology as Eschatology, ed. Frederick Herzog. New York: Herder and Herder, 1970, pp. 1-50.

_____. Theology of Hope, trans. James W. Leitch. New York: Harper and Row, 1967.

Mooney, Christopher F., S.J. Teilhard de Chardin and the Mystery of Christ. New York: Harper and Row, 1966.

_____. The Making of Man. Essays in the Christian Spirit. New York: Paulist Press, 1971.

Niebuhr, Reinhold. Does Civilization Need Religion? New York: The Macmillan Company, 1927.

O'Collins, Gerald G., S.J. Man and His New Hopes, New York: Herder and Herder, 1969.

_____. "Spes Quaerens Intellectum." Interpretation, 22, No. 1 (Jan., 1968), 36-52.

_____. "The Principle and Theology of Hope." Scottish Journal of Theology, 21, No. 2 (1968), 129-44.

Pannenberg, Wolfhart. Theology and the Kingdom of God. Phila.: Westminster Press, 1969.

Peters, Jan. "Black Theology as a Sign of Hope." Dimensions of Spirituality, Concilium Series, Vol. 59, ed. Christian Duquoc. New York: Herder and Herder, 1970, pp. 112-24.

Pieper, Josef. Hope and History, trans. Richard and Clara Winston. New York: Herder and Herder, 1969.

Pruyser, Paul W. A Dynamic Psychology of Religion. New York: Harper and Row, 1968.

_____. "Phenomenology and Dynamics of Hoping." Journal for the Scientific Study of Religion, III (Fall, 1963), 86-96.

Ramsey, Paul. Nine Modern Moralists. Englewood Cliffs, N.J.: Prentice-Hall, 1962.

Ruether, Rosemary. The Radical Kingdom: The Western Experience of Messianic Hope. New York: Harper and Row, 1970.

Schillebeeckx, Edward, O.P. God the Future of Man, trans. N. D. Smith. New York: Sheed and Ward, 1968.

Schoonenberg, Piet, S.J. Man and Sin, trans. Joseph Donceel, S.J. Chicago: Henry Regnery, 1965.

Springer, Robert H., S.J. "Conscience, Behavioral Science and Absolutes." Absolutes in Moral Theology?, ed. Charles E. Curran. Washington: Corpus Books, 1968, pp. 19-56.

Stern, E. Mark and Marino, Bert. G. Psychotheology. Paramus: Newman Press, 1970.

Teilhard de Chardin, Pierre. Building the Earth, trans. Nŏel Lindsay, Wilkes Barre: Dimension Books, 1965.

_____. Christianity and Evolution, trans. René Hague. New York: Harcourt Brace Jovanovich, Inc., 1971.

_____. Human Energy, trans. J. M. Cohen. New York: Harcourt Brace Jovanovich, Inc., 1971.

_____. Pierre Teilhard de Chardin-Maurice Blondel Correspondence. With Notes and Commentary by Henri de Lubac, S.J., trans. William Whitman. New York: Herder and Herder, 1967.

_____. Science and Christ, trans. René Hague. New York: Harper and Row, 1969.

_____. The Divine Milieu. New York: Harper Torchbooks, 1965.

_____. The Future of Man, trans. Norman Denny. New York: Harper Torchbooks, 1969.

_____. The Phenomenon of Man, trans. Bernard Wall. New York: Harper and Row Torchbooks, 2nd. ed., 1965.

_____. The Vision of the Past, trans. J. M. Cohen. New York: Harper and Row, 1966.

Thielicke, Helmut. Theological Ethics, ed. William H. Lazareth. Vol. 1 Foundations. Phila.: Fortress Press, 1966.

Tripole, Martin R., S.J. Community as Eschatology: An Investigation of the Theology of the Church of Jürgen Moltmann with a General Introduction to His Thought. An Unpublished Doctoral Dissertation Presented to Institut Catholique de Paris, May, 1972.

von Rad, Gerhard. Old Testament Theology, trans. D. M. G. Stalker. 2 Vols. New York: Harper and Row, 1962, 1965.

Wilder, Amos N. Eschatology and Ethics in the Teaching of Jesus. New York: Harper and Brothers, rev. ed., 1950.

Williams, Daniel Day. "Knowing and Hoping in the Christian Faith." The God Experience. Essays in Hope, ed. Joseph P. Whelan, S.J. New York: Newman Press, 1971, pp. 168-89.

ABOUT THE AUTHOR

Father Genovesi is an Associate Professor of Christian Ethics at Saint Joseph's University in Philadelphia. A native of this city, he entered the Maryland Province of the Society of Jesus in 1956. He holds graduate degrees from Fordham University and Woodstock College, and was ordained in 1969. He completed his doctoral studies in theology in 1973 at Emory University. Prior to his ordination he had taught philosophy at Loyola College in Baltimore. He has written for such journals as The American Ecclesiastical Review, The Way, America, The Thomist, Review for Religious, New Catholic World and the New Catholic Encyclopedia.